Primary Literacy Centers

Making Reading and Writing STICK!

Susan Nations and Mellissa Alonso

Maupin House

Primary Literacy Centers
Making Reading and Writing STICK

Cover design: *Maria Messenger*
Layout design: *Billie J. Hermansen*
Photographer: *Laurie MacDonald*

Library of Congress Cataloging-in-Publication Data

Nations, Susan.
  Primary Learning Centers : making reading and writing STICK! / Susan Nations, Mellissa Alonso,
    p. cm.
  Includes bibliographical references (p.) and index.
  ISBN 0-929895-46-0
    1. Language arts (Primary)--United States. 2. Classroom learning centers--United
States. I. Alonso, Mellissa, 1969- II. Title.
  Title.

LB1529.US N38 2000
372.6--dc21   00-065397

Contact both authors for inservice or consulting at www.literacycoaching.com or through the publisher.

Maupin House

Maupin House Publishing, Inc.
PO Box 90148
Gainesville, FL 32607
1-800-524-0634
www.maupinhouse.com

Publishing Professional Resources that Improve Classroom Performance

10 9 8 7 6 5 4 3 2

Table of Contents

Acknowledgements

We are so thankful for the many friends, colleagues and mentors who have supported the writing of this book! We would especially like to thank Dr. Brenda Parkes, for being there to talk to and encouraging us to take this leap. We are ever-grateful to Ginger, "the real thing," Summers for all your mentoring, coaching and inspiration. Our literacy journey began with you sharing your passion for teaching and learning with us. Thanks to Bob and Ann Scholl for encouraging us to take a risk and share our ideas with other literacy educators.

We are thankful for the children and teachers who allowed us to photograph them as they took part in centers: Suzi Boyett, Ashley Stafford, Julia Crawford, Nicole Crawford, Brianna Alonso, Jordan Nations, Nick Brooks, Cassie Funsch, Ben Billingsley, Andrew Guinart, Kedra Harvey, Khairi Watson, and Valerye Ramirez. Thank you for continuing to smile even when we say, "Just one more picture!" We are also grateful for Kristin Boerger, outstanding kindergarten teacher, who is always willing to share and give feedback to us.

From Mellissa:

I would first like to thank my husband, Hector and children, Brianna and Tony, for sharing me with my "writing partner" on many weekends. Your support and encouragement mean more to me than words can express.

Pam Locke and Susan Avery are the visionaries in Hillsborough County, where my journey as a reading teacher began. Your passion for reading is contagious. Thank you for sharing it with me. I am very proud of our Language Arts Team, for all they do to impact literacy in our district.

Barbara Ammirati, Cheri Middlebrooks and the staff of Temple Terrace Elementary, you will always be my first home. Thanks to my colleagues in Hillsborough County who challenge me to explore literacy in its greatest depth every day. You and your students are my teachers.

From Susan:

To my husband, Don for your willingness to dream big! I am thankful also, for my wonderful children, Daniel, Matthew, Jordan and Aaron because they allow me to wear so many different hats. You are special to me! To my extended family, thanks for your encouragement and interest in this project.

I also wish to thank my principal, Dr. Page Dettmann and the staff of Gocio Elementary School for continually thinking outside the box. Thank you for constantly seeking excellence for our children.

To Dr. Margie Wynn, Dr. Mary Virginia Peaslee, Dr. Beverly Wickson, Pam Locke, Karen Pierson, Debbie Arias, Tracye Brown, and Woodland Johnson, my wonderful professors and administrators who facilitated and encouraged my professional growth over the years.

Foreward

Two years ago, I was a member of the audience when Susan Nations and Mellissa Alonso presented a workshop that was the genesis of this book. Both of them were a little apprehensive that they might not draw an audience because their session was scheduled at a late time slot on the final day of the conference. In addition to this, the conference had been largely wiped out by the tail end of a hurricane which brought heavy rain and subsequent flooding. Despite all these factors, their fears were soon put to rest. The room was packed and remained so. When they finished the session to sustained applause, they were immediately surrounded by teachers who wanted to continue the dialogue. This was all testament not only to the high interest in the topic, but in their ability to connect with teachers at a highly practical level while grounding their ideas in a solid research base.

Primary Literacy Centers fulfills its early promise and will be a valuable addition to any teacher's professional resource collection whether they be beginning or seasoned teachers. Part One provides a clear road map for setting up, managing, and reviewing centers so that they become an integral part of the balanced literacy program. Mellissa

and Susan's experience as classroom teachers and staff developers shines throughout. You know as you read it and recognize how they help to avoid the pitfalls that can destroy the intent and purpose of center work, that they have truly walked their walk.

Part Two moves our thinking about the content and purpose of center work. This provides a clear opportunity for students to practice and internalize the strategies in independent and small group situations. By clearly showing the relationship between theory, explicit teaching, and related center activities Mellissa and Susan help teachers not only refine and extend their classroom practice, but to see where centers fit into the big picture of the overall classroom literacy program.

Both writers are avid learners who constantly question their theory and practice and how it affects the learners whose lives they touch. I know readers of this book, be they administrators, new or seasoned teachers, or parents will be enriched as they join Mellissa and Susan on their journey to find best practice for all children.

Dr. Brenda Parkes

PART ONE

Literacy Centers:
What, Why, and How

CHAPTER I

Introduction

An Overview of Balanced Literacy

Literacy Centers are an important element of a successful balanced literacy program. But literacy centers cannot "teach" students. They provide opportunities for practice and extension of skills and strategies taught in whole and small group. Instruction is ongoing and meaningful in the context of balanced literacy. The components of balanced literacy provide a framework of support as the student moves toward independently accessing and using strategies in reading and writing. A balanced literacy approach incorporates the following practices:

- Reading to, with and by students (Mooney, 1990)
- Connecting reading and writing
- Sharing quality literature and non-fiction
- Supporting readers with challenging text
- Matching readers to appropriate text
- Modeling decoding strategies and comprehension strategies
- Modeling thinking strategies and writing strategies
- Integrating reading, writing, listening, and speaking

Components of Readers' Workshop

Read Aloud: Reading aloud to students daily provides a model of fluency and builds listening comprehension. As the model, you read *to* the students *acting as the author and the reader* (Mooney, 1990). Students are released from the responsibility of concentrating on the mechanics of reading and are allowed to enjoy the text. Reading aloud may occur with the entire class, a small group, or an individual child.

Shared Reading: Shared reading mirrors the bedtime story situation when the reader and the child interact with the text (Holdaway, 1979). In the classroom, you read *with* the students as they interact with text that they cannot read for themselves (Mooney, 1990). This support allows active participation as you explicitly teach and model strategies for reading. Students have visual access to the text in the form of big books, charts, overhead transparency, etc. Shared reading may occur with the entire class, a small group, or an individual child.

Guided Reading: Guided reading provides a small group of students with the opportunity to talk, think and question their way through text (Mooney, 1990). Each student holds a copy of the text and the reading is done *by* the students as the teacher talks *with* the members of the group. Your role is to ensure an appropriate match between the students and the text by determining the supports and challenges within the text and the needs of the group.

Independent Reading: Independent reading occurs at all stages of reading development. Students assume full responsibility and know where to go for help when their comprehension breaks down. The reading occurs completely *by* the students and offers an opportunity for fluency building.

Components of Writers' Workshop

Modeled Writing: Modeled writing is a time for students to watch and listen as you think, talk and write about any topic. As you write, think aloud about strategies, conventions, ideas and language. This instructional opportunity places you, the teacher, in the role of an author. **You** hold the pen as **you** write about **your** ideas! Modeled writing usually occurs in front of the whole class.

Shared Writing: Shared writing encourages you and the students to collaborate on a piece of writing together. Students share ideas and you record them. Together you negotiate ideas, language and conventions about writing. **You** hold the pen and record contributions. Shared writing may occur with the entire class or a small group.

Another component of shared writing is **interactive writing**. During interactive writing, all of the elements of shared writing are present except for one. You **share** the pen with the students. As the text is constructed, call upon individuals to help you write a letter, word or sentence (depending upon their level of comfort). Interactive writing may occur with the entire class but is very effective with a small group of students.

Guided Writing: Guided writing follows the whole group lesson. This is the time for students to try out the skills and strategies you have modeled. As students write, you provide support and guidance through individual or small group conferences.

Independent Writing: Independent writing allows students to experiment, gain fluency and write freely. Sources of support such as word lists, word walls and/or dictionaries should be present for student use. Students should be explicitly taught when and how to use the resources in the room to assist them during this time.

The Role of Literacy Centers in Balanced Literacy

Literacy centers provide opportunities for students to practice skills and strategies that you have modeled and taught within the balanced literacy framework. Your centers will be more effective if the activities enhance and extend the literacy experiences students have engaged in during Readers' and Writers' Workshop. To assist your planning, we will connect all literacy center activities shared in this book to the components of Readers' and Writers' Workshop. This Strategy Teaching Cycle is illlustrated on page 5 and explained on page 27. This teaching cycle is like many others you have probably seen where you test—teach—practice—test, except it includes the opportunity for practice and application to take place within the context of literacy centers. The literacy center, therefore, must meet very specific criteria in order to be meaningful and effective for student learning.

What is a Literacy Center?

A literacy center is a place or activity that:

- Invites students to practice and apply strategies that have been taught and modeled in shared and guided literacy lessons

- Promotes reading, writing, speaking and viewing

- Allows students to manipulate language in both oral and written form

- Engages the learner through interaction

- Exposes students to a variety of text

- Provides open-ended activities for students

- Enables the teacher to assess and evaluate the students' use of literacy strategies

Cambourne's Conditions of Learning

How do children learn best? This question is the foundation of our learning and growing as professional educators. We often say children need to be engaged in their learning. Our goal as teachers is to make our classrooms inviting engaging places.

As we studied and read professional research, our classroom practice was impacted. Our study lead us to Dr. Brian Cambourne's research conducted in the 1970's on young children acquiring language. As a result of his research, he defined a set of conditions that must be present for the learner to be engaged and acquire any new skill. The conditions are: immersion, demonstration, expectation, employment, approximation, responsibility, and response.

This research set the stage for our rationale in using literacy centers to promote active engagement by students in the language arts classroom. There is no hierarchy of conditions. In *Invitations: Changing as Teachers and Learners K-12*, Regie Routman states, *They* (the conditions) *operate simultaneously in every successful...classroom and provide the context for language learning.* When these conditions are present, engagement of the learner occurs. Engagement should be the goal of every literacy-rich elementary classroom. Without it learning cannot take place. We list the conditions on page 7 with a definition and an example of what each might look like in the context of literacy centers.

How to Use This Book

This book is designed to help primary teachers—whether beginning or seasoned—consider ways to help students get the most out of the daily literacy instruction block. It is written in two parts. Part One is a how-to manual that also explains the rationale for using literacy centers. Because we want literacy strategies to "STICK" and stay with our students long after we introduce them, this section is divided into five parts and organized around the word "STICK" as follows:

- **S** – Strategy Immersion in Centers
- **T** – Tools that Target all Learners
- **I** – Increase Time in Text
- **C** – Choice not Chaos
- **K** – Keys to Success

Each of these sections is foundational for the successful set-up and use of literacy centers.

Part two is made up of 32 literacy connection planners that link readers' and writers' workshop instruction with center ideas. Each mini-lesson is designed using the Strategy Teaching Cycle introduced and explained on page 27 of section one.

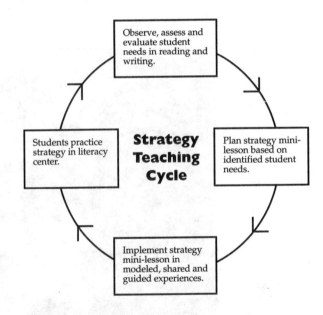

Observe, assess and evaluate student needs in reading and writing.

Plan strategy mini-lesson based on identified student needs.

Strategy Teaching Cycle

Students practice strategy in literacy center.

Implement strategy mini-lesson in modeled, shared and guided experiences.

The mini-lessons are focused on the skills and strategies children need to show proficiency in language arts. The center is the place where children practice and apply the skills and strategies they have learned. The literacy connection planner is designed to connect your whole and small group literacy instruction with the literacy center activities. Each literacy connection planner includes the following:

 Reading or ✏ Writing Strategy

✂ Materials

📁 Mini-lesson

✋ Literacy Center Connection

📋 Lesson Variations and Notes

Throughout the book we share stories of our own classroom experiences. These stories are found in boxes labeled "From Susan" or "From Mellissa". This will allow you, the reader, to know who is telling the story.

If you are new to centers, we suggest you spend time reading the first section that goes into great detail about how to get started. If you are just looking for some fresh ideas for an existing literacy center block, you may want to read section two first. See Appendix p. 209 for A Quick-Reference Guide to Finding Specific Center Acitivies in *Primary Literacy Centers.*

We know that the best ideas are those we get from a book or a fellow colleague then change to fit our own needs or the needs of our students. We invite you to make notes in this book as you read and consider how these centers can be used most effectively with your students.

Cambourne's Condition	What might it look like in a literacy center?
Immersion - The learner is surrounded with information about a topic.	• Provide a print-rich environment with words and labels around the classroom. • Immerse students with books and book talk. • Encourage children to talk to one another as they develop skills and strategies.
Demonstration - The learner is supported by by meaningful demonstrations of new tasks.	• Model for students BEFORE any activity is placed in a center • Explain the what, why and how of each task • Model process as well as product • Revisit demonstrations as needed
Expectation - The learner has an expectation that he can accomplish the task.	• Set up literacy centers in a supportive yet challenging manner. • Expect that learning will occur • Know what students CAN do
Employment (Use) - The learner needs time to practice for the skills to be developed. The learner makes decisions about what tasks will propel her forward in her learning	• Connect language arts mini-lessons to the literacy center experiences in the classroom • Give students many opportunities to practice and apply skills and strategies • Share the purpose of each activity
Approximation - The learner will take risks as he attempts new learning.	• Expect students will need many practice opportunities • Invite children to manipulate their language learning without expecting immediate mastery in centers • Value the process, not just the finished product • Place examples in centers to support student learning
Responsibility - The learner is given responsibility to make decisions about her learning.	• Set up centers so the learner can make meaningful decisions about reading and writing • Share the responsibility for new learning until students gain understanding • Allow for choice within centers • Teach and model expectations for center use
Response - The learner needs feedback about performance of a new task.	• Give feedback to the learning and activities that are generated in literacy centers • Invite students to positively respond to the work of peers • Encourage and inform students about their progress • Respond supportively and constructively

Engagement

CHAPTER 2

A Quick-Start Guide To Literacy Centers

Walk down any elementary school classroom during the first few weeks of school and you will hear, *We keep the _____ here, only use small dabs of glue, remember to put books back on the shelves neatly* or *we walk in our classroom.* Teachers are preparing their students to function in the classroom environment and be able to work independently. In *The First Days of School* classroom management consultant Harry Wong writes, *Student achievement at the end of the year is directly related to the degree to which the teacher establishes good control of the classroom procedures in the very first week of the school year.* A well-designed classroom helps everyone function better. When you plan for the physical space in your classroom, you must plan how you will familiarize students with acceptable movement, noise level, and use of materials. Many teachers want to rush the process of set up. Don't. Take time and model the use of centers as well as the use of materials within them. No matter when during the school year you read this book, you can make your learning environment optimal for you and your students by thinking carefully about your physical environment, management of materials and student responsibility during center time.

A List of Possible Literacy Centers and Their Purposes

Although many different centers can be set up in the elementary classroom, we recommend setting up seven literacy centers first. The centers we describe in *Primary Literacy Centers* will regenerate themselves throughout the year when you stock them with materials which encourage open-ended activities and allow student choice within them. As you plan your objectives and expectations for each literacy center, consider some of the supplies suggested in the Have It/Want It charts beginning on page 17 to encourage student-generated responses to reading and writing. These centers allow integration of content area materials, open-ended responses, as well as oral and written manipulation of language. See the following table listing all of the centers, along with their purposes.

Additional Centers

You may want to add other centers for your students during the literacy block. Many early childhood classrooms have other centers such as art, blocks, housekeeping, dramatic play, and math. If you are currently using any or all of these centers, as you read this book consider ways to bump up the level of literacy taking place within them.

Name of Center	Purpose
Classroom Library	Provides students with a variety of print and genre to practice reading skills and strategies.
Listening	Increases speaking, reading and writing vocabulary. Allows students to self-monitor fluency and progress in reading.
Literature Response	Gives students the opportunity to authentically respond to a text they have read or heard.
Poetry	Encourages students to read and perform various poems with fluency and expression. Exposes the struggling reader to rhyme, rhythm, and repetition.
Research	Integrates the study of science and social studies into the literacy hour. Provides children time to interact with non-fiction text.
Spelling/Word Work	Allows students to manipulate letters and words which can be integrated into their reading and writing experiences.
Writing	Provides opportunity for children to practice the writer's craft and target skills through self-selected topics and methods of presentation.

For example, you may want to add cookbooks, newspapers, phone books and notepads to housekeeping to simulate ways literacy is used in the home. Your block center may become a car repair shop where children write bills, read magazines and give estimates for work. There are many other ideas you will think of for adding literacy to traditional centers. After you decide how you will do this, consider which of the above literacy centers you would like to add to your classroom. A clear picture of what you want will help you as you continue to read this book.

Physical Environment

Decide which centers you will establish in your classroom and then plan for your physical environment. While there are many options for setting up a classroom, we suggest separating the noisier areas from those which require quiet more focused work. The centers where talking is important, such as writing, poetry, and research should be together to promote collaboration among students. Centers such as classroom library, listening, and literature response more often require participants to focus on their individual work and should be placed in areas of the room where quiet is respected. This will help minimize distractions for students as they complete their work.

Consider where you plan to conduct small group work while students are engaged in centers. Position yourself so you can conduct the small group effectively while monitoring student participation in centers. See pages 15-16 for two samples of primary classroom maps.

> **From Mellissa:**
>
> In the back of my classroom, I set up three small tables in a U-shape. This makes a cozy nook for small group work. The students sit facing me to keep them focused on the small group lesson. Positioning myself in the center allows me to interact with all the small group of students, as well as monitor the rest of my classroom center activities.

Acquiring Materials

A well-stocked center will be a busy and inviting place for students. The "Have It/ Want It" charts on pages 17-23 are designed to help you start thinking about materials you might want to include in your centers.

Student Responsibility

While a well-stocked center can be highly engaging, it can also break down when materials are misused, limited, or unfamiliar. Students must be taught to take responsibility for their learning environment before they can be expected to learn independently. Involving them in the process of set-up will help build a sense of ownership and community in your classroom. Teaching procedures for material use before opening any center for independent work will lead to a more successful learning experience for you and your students.

> **From Susan:**
>
> My first graders spent weeks learning how to click marker caps back on so they wouldn't dry out. I modeled it and we practiced together. I can still picture them sitting on the floor with markers right by their ears listening for the click. When they finally learned how, I let them use markers in centers.

Christine Saunders, teaches her kindergarten students this little rhyme: "If you don't hear it click, the marker will get sick!" Christine's students know that taking care of classroom supplies is everyone's responsibility. They understand that careful handling and use of materials allow them to continue to be able to use them during their center time. This type of modeling and practice is critical for student success in the center-oriented classroom.

Kids must know what is expected of them while they are in each center from simple tasks such as stapling papers together to how to clean up when they are finished. Demonstration is only the beginning of showing them what you want to happen during the work time. They must also practice the procedure with you. When you give them practice time, it allows you to see their level of understanding and make any changes necessary.

Carolyn Kelly, sets up centers with her first-grade students in a class meeting. In the beginning of the year, they sit together in an area she has designated for the center. Together they make a Looks Like/Sounds Like chart. She asks them to think about the center, the type of work that will go on there, and the way it will look and sound when being used properly. The students help generate a list of what the center should look like and sound like when in use.

Research Center	
Looks Like:	**Sounds Like:**
• Kids using tools carefully. • Recording our research. • Thinking about what we learn.	• Talking softly to a partner about our work. • Materials being moved around quietly. • Quiet voices.

Carolyn keeps the chart posted in the center. During the year she and her students refer to it and revise it to keep the center running smoothly. This repeated practice helps Carolyn's students know and understand her expectations of the learning environment.

When students demonstrate an understanding of the expectations within a center, you have the right and responsibility to let them know when it breaks down and to make changes as necessary. Occasionally make a list of all of those things that make you think your classroom is not running smoothly or that impede your students' learning process. Is it the student who uses 47 staples to put her book together? Is it the glue bottles left out with glue drying around them? Is it paper not stacked neatly when it is returned? Perhaps it's the student who is constantly tugging at your pants leg and asking, "What do I do now?" Have a class meeting to demonstrate and model what you expect your students to do during independent work time. You can expect to hold several class meetings throughout the year as problems arise.

Use some of your class meetings to talk about what would help your students function better in class. Let them share problems and suggest solutions at the class meeting. This helps them see that you are all a part of a learning community. It builds responsibility and begins to help them understand the

flexibility in the classroom environment. Most importantly, you are preparing your students to work independently while you teach small groups.

Teacher Tips for Successful Set Up

Following is a list of ideas for successful set up of literacy centers. These ideas have been collected from many of our colleagues based on their classroom experiences.

- **Clearly label supply bins and shelves** - Young children may need pictures or drawings of items that belong in each storage bin. Use a black marker and tagboard to make clear labels. Attach these labels to your bins and shelves using clear packaging tape. Students will be able to look around your room and see very clearly where you expect items to be put away after use.

- **Establish clear boundaries for your centers** - Your students must be able to understand where each center begins and ends. Use your classroom furniture, rugs, hula hoops or appliance boxes to section off spaces for each center. Place a label or icon in the center so your students will be able to identify it. When you decide where each center will be, sit in the chair you will use in your small group space and be sure you have clear visual access to student activity.

- **Open one center at a time** - When you are first beginning centers only open one at a time until you know that your students understand the routines and procedures required for proper use. Allow children to rotate to and from the center in a shortened center time called trial time. Be sure to discuss as a class what goes well and what needs improvement. Add to or change your Looks Like/ Sounds Like charts.

- **Create a center management chart/ rotation** - Several center management charts are explained on pages 13 and 14. Help your students understand your system in the beginning so they know exactly where they should be during literacy center time.

- **Minimize teacher interruptions** - Mellissa designates center captains in her room. She selects students who know and understand what should be happening within each center. Each of these students wears a clothespin during center time. Other classmates know when they have a question they must go ask the center captain. If the captain is unable to answer the question he may go ask Mellissa. Since this is the only person allowed "teacher access" during small groups, it minimizes distractions from other students.

- **Determine a signal for clean-up time** - It is hard for young children to just stop what they are doing. Help them prepare to stop by giving a five-minute warning. Many teachers use a bell or sing a song when it is time to clean up centers. Whatever signal you choose, use it consistently so your children understand that they must stop what they are doing and clean up.

Maximizing Space

Space for centers is limited in some classrooms. While some centers may be at designated tables, shelves or corners around the perimeter of the classroom, others may be stored in plastic tubs or bags which are placed on student desks during literacy center time. Here are some suggestions to help you maximize your space:

- **Gift Bags** - Store centers in gift bags. Students can bring the bag to their seat during literacy center time. One teacher fills the bag with books related to the pictures on the outside. For example, a fish bag would be filled with fiction and non-fiction books about the ocean, ocean word cards to alphabetize, fish stamps and stickers to write about the ocean, and poetry cards with fish pointers for fluency building.

- **Child's Lunch Boxes** - You can store center activities and supplies in children's lunch boxes. These can often be found at garage sales at very low cost.

- **Cereal Boxes** - Collect empty cereal boxes from your students. Cut the box as shown in the diagram. Use these boxes to store small books, magazines, and small pointers for book browsing.

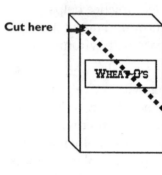
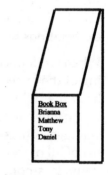

- **Miniature Garbage Cans** - Miniature garbage cans can be found at the dollar store. You can also use one-gallon ice cream buckets for cans. Place these in each center for students to throw away their small scraps. Make emptying the trash part of your daily center clean up. This will minimize the movement across your classroom to discard trash and keep your centers tidy.

- **Shoe Boxes** - Shoe boxes, either cardboard or plastic, make great center containers. They can be moved to a student desk or floor space for students to work during literacy center time.

- **Clothesline** - Attach a clothesline under your chalk tray. Store centers in plastic storage bags and clip them to the line. When students are ready to work in centers, they can go get a bag and take it to a designated work area.

- **Hula Hoops** - Hula Hoops spread out on the floor make nice center work space. Children know exactly where the boundaries are. The materials also stay in one place.

Managing Centers

Many teachers start centers without a clear management system. Don't. If you want centers to run smoothly, good management is critical. Decide important questions regarding your literacy centers before you start. Should students visit each center daily? Weekly? Bi-weekly? How will I monitor my students' use of centers? How do I want children to move during the literacy center time?

A clear, understandable center organization will help your students know exactly what you expect. Below you will find some ideas for managing student movement during center time. Try one or two to find the one that's right for you. You will have to model how to read and interpret this chart many times with your students. Once they get it, it will help you be able to pull small groups without worrying whether or not they are following your directions.

We have provided center icons for you on pages 194-203 of the appendix. These can be used to create any of the center management systems listed below.

Management Board

Cluster your centers into groups of two or three. Below each cluster, place a list of five or six children. Rotate the lists each day to a new cluster of centers. Place your chart at the children's eye level and in a place where they can refer to it as they move through their assigned centers.

Pocket Chart

Use the pocket chart much the same way you would the management board. Write each student's name on an index card. Group students next to the center or centers they should complete that day. You will need to provide some options in case students finish their work in their assigned center. Some options might include: read a book, write a letter, read or write in your journal, read the room, listening center, etc.

Second grade teacher, *Cathy Corona,* puts a bright colored index card behind one student's name for each center on her pocket chart. This is the designated center captain who is responsible for seeing that the materials are being used properly. The captain also checks to see that the center is cleaned up at the end of center time.

Center Contract

Provide each student with a contract. As they work in a center, they record it on their contract. Some teachers like to follow this up with a daily learning log where students write what they did during center time and their plans for next time. (See pages 24 and 25)

Work Wheel

This system works like the management board. Place icons on a large cardboard pizza wheel divided into four sections. Write each student's name on a clothespin. Each day, attach the clothespin to the wheel showing where each child should work. Rotate the clothespins daily.

Use this information, and the space below, to design your own center management system.

Name of Center	# of Students	Location in Room	Quiet or Talking?	How often will they visit?	Product or Process?	Do I have materials?

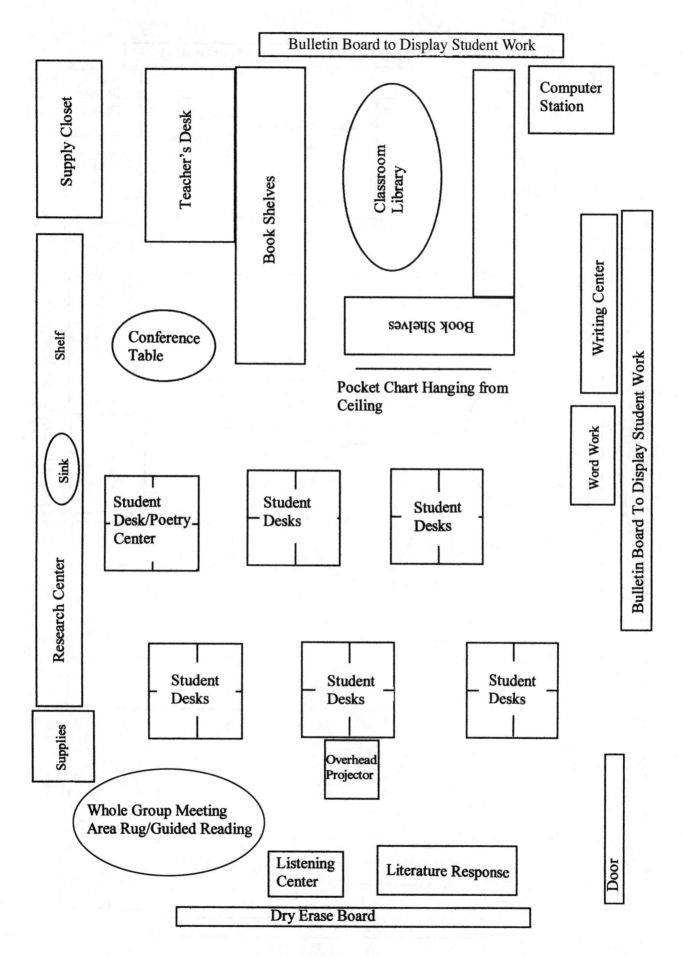

Bulletin Board to Display Student Work

Supply Closet

Teacher's Desk

Book Shelves

Classroom Library

Computer Station

Shelf

Conference Table

Book Shelves

Writing Center

Pocket Chart Hanging from Ceiling

Sink

Word Work

Research Center

Student Desk/Poetry Center

Student Desks

Student Desks

Bulletin Board To Display Student Work

Supplies

Student Desks

Student Desks

Student Desks

Overhead Projector

Whole Group Meeting Area Rug/Guided Reading

Door

Listening Center

Literature Response

Dry Erase Board

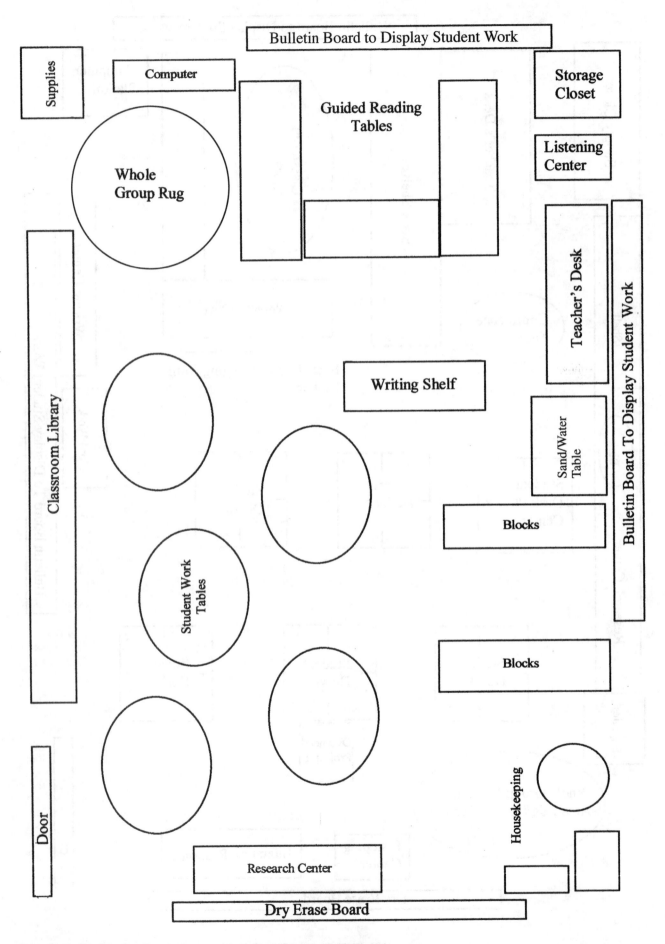

Bulletin Board to Display Student Work

Supplies

Computer

Storage Closet

Guided Reading Tables

Whole Group Rug

Listening Center

Classroom Library

Teacher's Desk

Writing Shelf

Bulletin Board To Display Student Work

Sand/Water Table

Blocks

Student Work Tables

Blocks

Door

Housekeeping

Research Center

Dry Erase Board

Classroom Library

Have It	Want It	Material Name	Description/Notes
		books	The classroom library should be stocked with fiction and non-fiction books at a variety of reading levels.
		class-made books	Honor student work by placing class produced books in your library.
		magazines	Keep a bin of magazines for kids. After they have read these, they can cut out the pictures to place in the writing center.
		newspapers	Check with your local paper to see about their Newspapers in Education program.
		comfortable pillows or chairs	Place bean bags, large pillows, or child-sized chairs in your library to provide a comfortable place to read.
		bins for storage	Organize your books by author, topic, illustrator, etc. Label for easy student accessibility.
		shelves	When possible, turn some books so that the covers are displayed rather than the spines.
		labels for bins and shelves	Labels can be made by author, genre or difficulty of book. Use colored dots on the labels and place the corresponding colored dot on the book spine for easy reorganization.
		class-generated writing charts	Students love to re-read their own writing. Keep these charts at eye level for students to revisit in your library.
		reading glasses	Use old sunglasses with the lenses popped out. Students love to wear glasses when they read.
		pointers	Keep a bucket of pointers handy for students as they reread charts, big books, poems, etc.
		lamps	Lamps add a cozy touch to a reading corner.
		carpet	Carpet squares or a large area rug add comfortable boundaries to the library space.

Listening

Have It	Want It	Material Name	Description/Notes
		books or poems on tape	Many publishers produce tapes to accompany their books.
		baskets or plastic bins to organize book selections	Place the book and audiotape in a gallon-size resealable bag. Label each piece with a colored dot for easy clean-up.
		cassette player	Label the buttons on your cassette player as follows: green dot = play, red dot = stop. Mark the volume dial with a line of white out to keep the volume under control.
		blank audio cassettes	Use for students to record their own reading. Place in the student portfolio for assessment and evaluation. Parents can listen to this tape during conferences with you.
		Language Master	Purchase prerecorded cards or record your own.
		paper for response	Add writing to the listening center by having students write a response to a book. (i.e. draw or write a retelling, tell your favorite part, write what you learned etc.)
		pencils, pens, markers, crayons	Cover and label empty juice cans for storage. Keep a can of sharpened pencils available for students to trade in broken ones.
		baby wipes	Keep disposable baby cloths on hand to clean earphones after use.
		film strip viewer	Many media centers have old individual film strip viewers. Use these for students to listen and view at this center.
		individual cassette players	Students can use these instead of the larger listening center.
		listening log	Have students keep a reading log posted at the reading center of books they have heard.

Literature Response

Have It	Want It	Material Name	Description/Notes
		books	Use familiar shared or guided reading text for students to revisit as they respond.
		magazines	Students can locate an interesting picture or article and write a response. Older readers may want to submit an editorial to the magazine.
		literature response matrix	See page 35. Students choose a response idea from the matrix to complete after reading.
		paper	Supply paper in a variety of sizes and colors to encourage creative response.
		scissors, glue, tape, stapler	Discount stores often have inexpensive tubs which can be used to organize these items.
		schema connection chart	Students make connections between what they read and what they know. See page 81.
		journals	Students respond to reading through their writing. They can dialogue with another student, write to a character, tell a favorite part, etc.
		markers, crayons, pencils, pens	Organize into cans or bins for easy access.
		sticky notes	As students revisit text, they can add sticky notes to pages which make them think, feel or remember something.
		inquiry questions	Post question stems (see page 85) for students to use in their response journals.
		critic review board	Have students write a critique of a book or article they have read. Post these in the response center.

Poetry

Have It	Want It	Material Name	Description/Notes
		books of poems	Label by author, topics, anthologies, etc.
		poetry charts	Purchase from educational suppliers or create your own on chart paper.
		interactive file folder poems	Convert interactive chart poems to smaller file folders for individual student use.
		computer-generated poems	Use your desk-top publisher to illustrate poetry from shared and guided reading.
		pocket chart	Write poems on sentence strips and place in a pocket chart for students to order and innovate.
		overhead projector	Copy familiar poems onto overhead transparencies. Students can use pointers and over head pens to read, illustrate or innovate poems. Store these poems in a three ring binder near your overhead projector.
		pointers	Keep a can of small and large pointers for students to track print in the poetry center.
		class poetry notebook	As you read poems together, compile a notebook of favorites for students to revisit throughout the year.
		magnetic poetry word cards	Purchase or create your own magnetic poetry words. Students can use these words to compose their own poems.
		individual poetry notebooks	Copy familiar poems on small paper. Students choose one poem each week to insert and illustrate in their own poetry notebook. Have students use tape or a glue stick to attach their poems. This keeps the pages from sticking together.
		pens, pencils, highlighters	Students can revisit poems in their notebooks and highlight rhyming words, strong verbs, word patterns, etc.
		tape	Use to affix poems inside notebook.
		scissors	Use your storage can to display beautiful language you have read or words you want your students to remember.

Research

Have It	Want It	Material Name	Description/Notes
		nonfiction books	Keep books clearly labeled and organized by theme, topic, or author in bins or baskets.
		maps	Get laminated maps from your local insurance agent.
		attraction/travel brochures	Use brochures found in local hotels, restaurants, and travel agencies.
		sorting bin	A kitchen relish tray with several compartments works well for this. Students can sort and classify different items related to topic of study. (See page 180)
		magnifying glasses, a balance, rulers, and tweezers	Keep these items available for students to use when observing, classifying, and sorting items in the research center.
		properties chart	List attributes (colors, size, shape, weight, etc.) on a chart. Have students describe the object in an observation log.
		pens, pencils, and markers, highlighters	Students need a variety of writing utensils to record their observations in the center.
		inquiry chart	Write several question stems on a chart. (see page 85) Students can use this chart as they record their thinking and observations at this center.
		empty food boxes	Create question cards to accompany familiar food boxes. (See page 158)
		observation sheets	Students can use a clipboard and glasses as they record their observations and investigations at this center.
		thematic vocabulary charts or word rings	Keep specialized or thematic vocabulary organized on charts, in a file folder, or on index cards bound with a ring. (Label with stickers, photos, or pictures for younger students)
		nonfiction magazines and newspapers	Provide a basket of children's magazines and newspapers to promote independent study of high interest topics.
		clipboards	Use with observation sheets and other scientific investigations.

Spelling/Word Work Center

Have It	Want It	Material Name	Description/Notes
		letter tiles	These can be made using one-inch square ceramic tiles from the home improvement store. Write a letter on each tile using permanent marker. Use blue for consonants and red for vowels. Protect them using clear nail polish.
		plastic or foam letters	Use these for sorting, making words, and student exploration.
		magnetic letters	Aluminum cookie sheets work well for practicing using letters and words. Letters can also be stored in cookie tins. The lids of the tins double as a workboard.
		dry erase boards and markers	Students can write and notice word patterns and sounds within words. Purchase kitchen backsplash at your local home improvement center and have it cut to 12"x18".
		word cards	Use the pictures from old workbooks, worksheets, or magazines to make illustrated word cards for students to sort.
		rubber letter stamps	Students can use the letter stamps to make word family lists, reproduce spelling lists, and/or work with word patterns.
		magic slates, magna doodles	Use to practice letter formation, word patterns, spelling, etc.
		letter sorting cans	Margarine tubs or juice cans labeled with letters or word patterns for sorting small toys and trinkets.
		paper, Post-It notes, writing tools	Keep plenty of these supplies on hand to encourage students to try out new words, patterns, or sounds.
		Wikki Sticks, pipe cleaners, play dough/clay	Use to form letters and words. Wikki Sticks can be stored on vinyl placemats.
		alphabet macaroni or cereal	Glue onto index cards to make words and sentences.
		newspapers, dictionary, thesaurus	Students must know how to use reference materials to locate and explore unknown words and meanings.

Writing

Have It	Want It	Material Name	Description/Notes
		variety of paper	Provide a wide variety of shapes, colors, and sizes to keep student interest while working in the center.
		blank books	Use wallpaper sample books for covers. Staple 4-6 sheets of paper folded in half inside.
		writing tools	Provide a variety of pens, pencils, crayons and markers for student writing.
		staplers	Model how to use one or two staples to attach papers.
		hole punch, paper clips, tape, highlighters	Students can use these supplies to create small books, edit or organize materials
		dry erase white boards	Purchase kitchen backsplash at the home improvement center and have it cut to 12"x18."
		rubber stamps, pads, and stickers	Picture stamps, stickers and letter stamps can help children with illustrating and composing.
		envelopes	Ask greeting card companies and print shops to donate envelopes to your classroom.
		clipboards	Clipboards free students to work in comfortable corners of the room.
		writing idea file and/or picture file	Keep a list of topics to write about for students to reference. The picture file is a springboard for student writing ideas.
		mini-dictionaries	Made from stickers,worksheets, computer icons, etc.
		dictionary/ thesaurus	Make sure these are age-appropriate and user-friendly.
		word wall	Word walls should be displayed for easy physical access during writing. (See personal word walls pages 133-135).
		computer	Use for publishing student writing.
		thematic vocabulary chart	Use stickers, old worksheets, or magazines to make a chart of thematic vocabulary. Keep this posted during the entire unit to encourage use of these words in writing.

My Name: _____

Center Names	Mon.	Tues.	Wed.	Thurs.	Fri.
Listening					
Literature Response					
Poetry					
Reading					
Read the Room					
Research					
Word Work					
Writing					
My Free Choice This Week: _____					

_____'s Independent Learning Log

Date	Name of Center	What I did today…	Evidence of my learning…a product, a friend's initials, etc.	Reflections on My Learning How can this help me in other areas?

CHAPTER 3

Strategy Immersion in Centers

Tools That Target All Learners

Increase Time In Text

Choice Not Chaos

Keys to Success

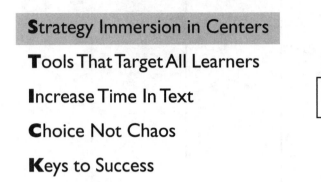

A strategy is a tool or technique students use when reading or writing to help move them toward fluency and understanding. The strategies identified in this book are broad and encompass several instructional opportunities. They are based on the National Council of Teachers of English and International Reading Association (NCTE/IRA) List of Standards for the English Language Arts. These standards are listed in the Appendix on pages 187-188. Literacy curricula designed and implemented across the country use these standards and strategies. In a balanced literacy framework, reading strategies are modeled during read aloud and shared reading lessons. Students practice strategies during guided reading with teacher support. Likewise, teachers demonstrate writing strategies during modeled and shared writing, while guided and independent writing provide students time to practice. With literacy demands higher than ever before, it is critical that we give students time to practice and apply the strategies we teach. Literacy centers are a valuable extension of these experiences because they provide authentic opportunities for students to practice and apply reading and writing strategies.

In many classrooms the question that often initiates centers is, *How can I keep the kids busy while I'm teaching a small group lesson?* As a result of such thinking, centers are in danger of becoming glorified board work having no

real meaning for kids. How many teachers spent years cutting, coloring, laminating and re-cutting games to be put into centers with little or no purpose? These were usually filled with isolated skills and failed to help children learn to read and write better. Transfer of these skills was sporadic at best because students did not utilize them in real reading and writing situations. Sometimes the only reason a skill appeared on center games was because it was in a scope and sequence somewhere. The skill had little or nothing to do with assessment and evaluation, the developmental stages of students, or their literacy needs. The centers in *Primary Literacy Centers* are designed to provide students ongoing meaningful practice because they are directly connected to your literacy instruction.

Within the balanced literacy framework, teachers demonstrate new skills and strategies through focused mini-lessons. Mini-lessons are brief modeling sessions (10-15 minutes) designed to introduce or reinforce a specific literacy skill or strategy. An effective mini-lesson connects students' background experiences with new learning. In *Endangered Minds*, Jane M. Healy says, *One of the biggest gaps in children's experiences these days is in seeing connections between all the bits of information they have accumulated...* Therefore, connections must be made between assessment, planning, teaching mini-lessons and the literacy center experience. We call this the Strategy Teaching Cycle.

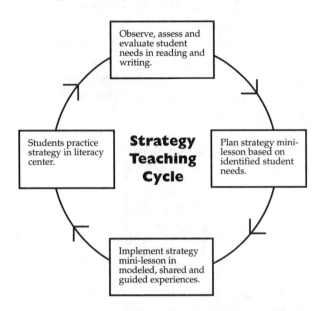

Now the question that should drive center activity is, *How will this literacy center reinforce my mini-lesson(s)?*

Identify a Strategy

When you use the strategy teaching cycle, begin by identifying a focus strategy. Below, we define eight reading and writing strategies that help move students toward fluency. Table 1 defines and connects these reading and writing strategies. Each definition is followed by the NCTE/IRA Standard correlation. Under each definition are strategic behaviors which we know good readers and writers use when they employ the strategy. Use the list as a menu of specific literacy behaviors you will model for your students.

Table 1

Reading Strategies	Writing Strategies
Strategies for Comprehension - readers construct meaning from a variety of text. • using prior knowledge to interact with text • confirming/revising predictions about text • rereading to self-monitor for comprehension • summarizing information from text (NCTE/IRA Standard 3)	**Strategies for Communicating a Message** - writers construct text for a variety of purposes • selecting an appropriate form of writing with an audience in mind • checking for meaning using self-monitoring strategies (rereading, revising for understanding) (NCTE/IRA Standard 5)
Strategies for Learning and Using Words - readers use their understanding of word identification and meaning during text interaction. • using sound/symbol relationships to identify new words • using word families/word patterns to identify new words • using context cues or word structures to construct meaning • using resources and references to build vocabulary (dictionary, thesaurus, word wall, peers, etc.) (NCTE/IRA Standard 3)	**Strategies for Word Choice** - writers use their understanding of words and their meaning to make effective word choices. • choosing clear and specific words to convey meaning to an audience • engaging the reader using descriptive details • using models of literature as a source for understanding word choice • revising word choice to build understanding for the reader (NCTE/IRA Standard 4)
Strategies for Finding Information - readers gather, evaluate, and synthesize data from a variety of sources. • selecting and organizing information from text. • using textual information to support an answer (NCTE/IRA Standard 7)	**Strategies for Using Information** - writers communicate their discoveries for a variety of purposes and audiences. • organizing information to present to an audience • recording observations using descriptive details (NCTE/IRA Standard 7)
Strategies for Building Fluency and Independence - readers self-select appropriate text and read for a variety of purposes • attending to punctuation and reading in whole phrases rather than word by word • reading with expression and intonation • reinforcing sentence syntax by murmur reading (NCTE/IRA Standard 12)	**Strategies for Building Fluency and Independence** - writers self-select topics and write for a variety of purposes • using prior knowledge of the topic to write with fluency • making choices regarding publication • reinforcing sentence syntax using edit-by-ear technique (NCTE/IRA Standard 12)

Many school districts and state departments of education have identified expectations or standards for the language arts based on the NCTE/IRA standards. We encourage you to check your local district or state department expectations and/or standards. Once you identify them, then you are ready to begin the Strategy Teaching Cycle.

Observe/Assess/Evaluate

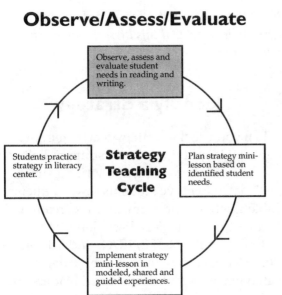

Before teaching a strategy, you must observe, assess, and evaluate what your students already know and are able to do. Then work from your students' strengths, not their weaknesses. One helpful way to focus on strengths is to note student behaviors you observe during language arts. Some assessment opportunities within balanced literacy may include:

Records of Oral Reading
Oral and Written Retellings
Taped Readings
Writing Samples
Writing Conferences

Although most of the strategies students employ during reading and writing are what Marie Clay calls "in the head" type strategies, sometimes they are easily clarified by conducting a brief conference. Below you will find suggestions for observing and recording student use of strategies in whole and small group settings. These are only suggestions. We have found that teachers have many methods of record keeping. You will need to find the method that works for you. The important thing is once you have found a way, *stay* with it! Your records are evidence of a student's growth in your class. These records often reveal a more complete picture of the student as a learner than the traditional progress report.

Clipboard Comments: Write or print your students' names on a sheet of address labels purchased from an office supply center. Record student behaviors (i.e. reads left to right, uses strong verbs) during reading and writing. Date stamp the labels then peel and place in individual files. This system is nice for assuring you observe all children within the language arts block.

Student Sign Up Chart: You can have students sign up to conference with you during the workshop time. As you talk with the individual student, make notes on an index card or sticky note to be placed in the student's portfolio or observation chart.

> I need a reading
> conference:
>
> Jordan ✓
> Dagny
> Logan
> Aaron
> Michelle

Daily Workshop Focus Groups: Divide your class into four groups. Label a file folder with the days of the week Monday through Thursday. Identify one group for each day. On the inside left of the file folder tape index cards labeled at the bottom with each students name in one focus group. Repeat this for the right side as well. Keep the names the same on both sides of the file folder so each student has two cards labeled with her name. Title one side *Behaviors Observed*. Label the other side *Teaching Points*. On Monday, you will observe and focus on Monday's group. These are the students you will plan to conference with during workshop time. Using this system, you will have time with each student at least once a week. Use Friday to catch up with any students who were absent or who need extra attention.

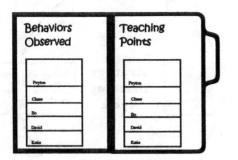

Observation Checklists: Many textbook publishers and professional book authors have created observation checklists. These are often based on the NCTE/IRA standards and are wonderful tools for organization and observation. Several sources of these check- lists are listed in the bibliography.

Sometimes you can only guess what the child is doing when he decodes a word in context or takes part in the writing process. Did he use graphophonics, context, syntax or all of the cueing systems when reading the text? Is she using craft she has noticed in other text? Does her piece have logical flow? Learn to become kid watchers so you can make some educated decisions about your students' reading and writing behaviors. The empha- sis should be on moving the child forward in the use of skills and strategies. Once you begin truly watching your students, you will know which strategies to introduce and when they are appropriate.

Plan Targeted Mini-Lesson

Observe, assess and evaluate student needs in reading and writing.

Students practice strategy in literacy center.

Strategy Teaching Cycle

Plan strategy mini- lesson based on identified student needs.

Implement strategy mini-lesson in modeled, shared and guided experiences.

Your assessments and observations will help you plan to teach your selected strategy. Consider what your students need to know in order to move ahead in their understand- ing. Plan your mini-lesson within the context of the balanced literacy framework. Decide whether the lesson should be delivered in modeled, shared or guided experiences.

The Literacy Connection Planners in *Primary Literacy Centers* always begin with a mini- lesson focused on a skill or strategy students need to move forward in their learning. Our lessons show examples of mini-lessons connected to strategies. Use these lessons as models to help you plan your own mini- lessons based on your students' needs.

Implement Mini-Lesson

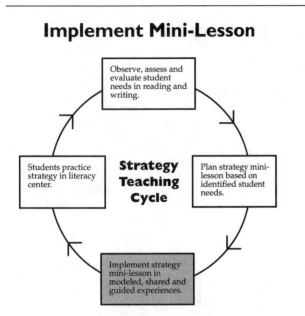

Once you have planned the mini-lesson you are ready to deliver it. Remember that a mini-lesson is a brief investigation into a particular teaching point. In primary classrooms, these are lessons that will spiral throughout the year. There is no need to over-do any one teaching point as you will have many opportunities to revisit it.

Sometimes you will have only a few students who need the mini-lesson skill or strategy. Conduct these lessons during small group teaching. These skills and strategies can still be practiced within the context of a literacy center. When you teach to the whole group, make sure that a majority of the students need the lesson. If you teach a mini-lesson on punctuation when most of your class does not need it, you will lose those students.

Practice and Apply in Literacy Centers

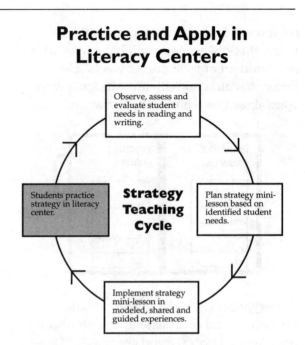

Children must be given time to practice and apply any new skill or strategy before they are evaluated on it. Be careful to make this practice risk-free. When we give our students meaningful practice in literacy centers, then the skill can become a strategy that students can access when needed.

It is easy to want to skip this step. We tend to think that our young students need us 100% of the time. What they need is for us to let go and let them try. Picture yourself learning to drive. If you never took the car out on your own, you would not be a skilled driver. The same is true of your students, they need time on their own to try out their new learning. This practice time is critical to their growth as literacy learners.

The second part of this book describes sample mini-lessons and literacy center connections using the eight reading and writing strategies from Table 1. Following each lesson is a list of possible lesson variations to meet the needs of learners across grade levels and/or developmental stages. You will also find a blank planner to assist you in connecting your language arts mini-lessons to your literacy centers.

CHAPTER 4

Strategy Immersion in Centers

Tools That Target All Learners

Increase Time In Text

Choice Not Chaos

Keys to Success

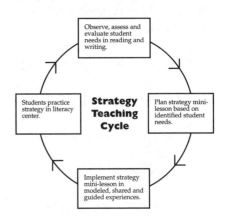

In classrooms where the students are grouped heterogeneously, it is difficult to make sure the work at centers will target the specific needs of all learners. How do you make sure that the above-level reader is experiencing some challenge in the work while the at-risk reader is not frustrated with the work? Both situations can lead to discipline problems. Rather than staying on task, the frustrated or bored learner often becomes a distraction and causes the rest of the learning environment to be less than optimal. In this chapter, we provide suggestions that will help you make learning centers high-quality learner-centered activities.

Understand Students' Zone of Proximal Development (ZPD)

Providing a high level of choice within your literacy centers gives each of your students the opportunity to construct learning at their individual learning level as well as allow them to collaborate with peers. Russian psychologist, Lev Vygotsky, identifies this collaborative construction of learning as the zone of proximal development or ZPD. Vygotsky maintains that *the child follows the example of an adult or 'more capable peers' and gradually develops the ability to do certain tasks without help or assistance.* This is the goal of the literacy center. Students need to have

time to practice in their zone in order to gain understanding, yet need to be encouraged to move toward using skills and strategies independently. The ZPD applies to *any activity in which individuals are in the process of developing knowledge*. It is not necessary for an adult teacher to be present for children to operate in their ZPD as peers can provide the support or assistance to the learner.

Provide Text at a Variety of Levels Within Centers

When you present a small or whole group strategy mini-lesson, model it in text that is on grade level and familiar to your students. Your students will be able to focus on the skill or strategy lesson better if they already have some control of the print and comfort with the message. When possible, provide text in the centers that is above and below the level of demonstration for students to use when they practice the skill or strategy in their own zone of proximal development. For example, if you teach a lesson on determining author's purpose for reading you will want to demonstrate this using on-grade level familiar text. At the literature response center, provide books that cover the reading levels of all readers in your classroom. This allows all readers to experience success within their zone of proximal development.

Kristin Boerger, kindergarten teacher and reading coach, color codes activities within her centers. This is done easily by applying a sticky dot label on the center activity. Students know that activities with a red dot are going to be a challenge, while activities with a yellow one are in the middle, and those with a green dot are easier still.

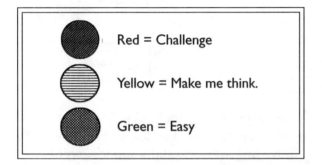

Red = Challenge

Yellow = Make me think.

Green = Easy

Kristin's students can choose the level of difficulty they want to work at while they are in the center. This leveling system also allows her to monitor her students' progress while keeping them challenged and motivated to work in centers. She redirects those students who continue to complete the easier centers but need more challenge. Kristin can easily point individual students toward the activity that will provide optimal learning for each task.

The literature response center is a good example of one in which children can function at their individual levels yet have common types of responses. Students work at this center in response to their independent or guided reading. This is a center stocked with materials and suggestions for responding to literature both during and after student reading. The purpose is to allow students choice in responding while still checking for their understanding of the text they are reading. On page 35 is a sample of a response matrix that hangs in the literature response center. Model with your students each of the responses. Over time they will be able to self-select a response to show their understanding of a text. Explanations of the matrix responses are located in the appendix pages 204-205.

The centers in *Primary Literacey Centers* are designed to help you provide activities that allow children to learn both cooperatively and independently. You will find many more examples of centers that target all learners in the Literacy Center Connection Planners in Part Two.

Set up Heterogeneous Groups

We recommend that you do not group students in their guided reading groups for the center time. This can impede learning at centers if there are no models for the struggling readers. Grouping students in heterogeneous groups gives your students a support system to complete their work in literacy centers. The levels of students within a typical primary classroom vary greatly. Setting up heterogeneous groups helps students learn to appreciate the strengths of center group members. This allows students who are working below level to have fluent models in their peers. It also keeps those leaders in the class from all working together. The old adage, *too many chefs spoil the soup* can ring true when there are too many leaders trying to control what is happening within the center.

Grouping should be flexible enough that you can change membership when necessary. It is important for you to be able to work as a professional in your classroom. Therefore, when behavior during center time keeps you from working with a small group, it is your job to reevaluate and consider new grouping solutions. (See diagram of grouping possibilities on page 33).

Flexible Grouping

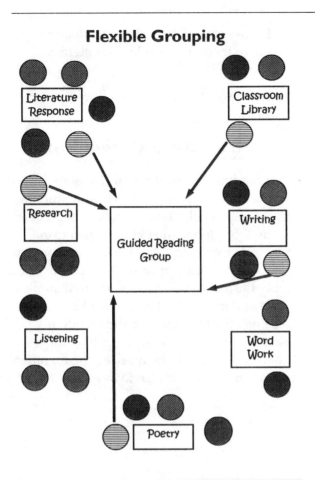

Use Open-ended Activities

Your literacy centers should be filled with open-ended activities and models such as the literature response center described above. We must not limit our children's potential by making the work we give them too closed-ended. Many teachers do this and wonder why their students are losing interest so quickly in centers. Not only will the open-ended activities keep your students interested in their work, it will also perpetuate new learning among them. Kids are remarkably able to rise above what we often think they can do.

From Mellissa:

I remember watching a kindergarten teacher introduce the idea of the retelling box (see Literature Response Matrix page 35) to a group of her students. They thought the idea was OK and used it once or twice, but asked permission to do their own type of retelling. Before she knew it they were retelling their stories by writing their own puppet plays! Think about what would have happened if the teacher had told them, "No, you must do it my way!" Imagine the learning they would have lost!

Display Student Samples

We suggest you display student work samples in centers around your room. Students can learn so much from seeing work generated by their peers. These displays both validate the learning that is taking place in literacy centers and continue to help build community in the classroom. Students who are challenged by center activities will have models to use in their responses. Change these displays frequently so your students will always have fresh ideas to use in their work.

From Susan:

I remember teaching Dustin, an awkward first grader and a struggling reader. The other kids in my classroom knew that reading was a chore for him and often could be heard reading to him. His peers quickly learned that Dustin was an incredible artist. He could draw things with much more detail than most of the rest of the class. Soon after their discovery they could be heard asking Dustin to illustrate their writing. This type of collaboration acknowledged Dustin as an important part of our classroom community. Before the year was over, Dustin was reading very close to his peers and they were drawing with much more precision. What happened in that classroom would not have happened if Dustin had never been exposed to readers above his level.

Keep Center Activity Meaningful to Students

When you introduce a new skill or strategy lesson be sure it is one your students need. Management of centers often breaks down when students are asked to complete tasks that will not move them forward in their literacy and have no real meaning for them. As you consider mini-lessons to use with your class, ask yourself the following questions:

• Who needs this mini-lesson?

• In which part of balanced literacy will I introduce this lesson?

• When do I expect my students to use this skill or strategy?

• How will my students practice and apply this skill/strategy in literacy centers?

• Why did I choose this skill or strategy to introduce/reinforce?

• Do my students need this strategy to move them forward in their literacy learning?

• What will my model look like?

Fill a Student's Tool Box

Your reading and writing mini-lessons should always attempt to give your students more tools to help them in their pursuit of literacy. Students must know when to employ the proper strategy. Each time you give your students the opportunity to practice and apply the skills and strategies you demonstrate and model, you will move them closer to being able to determine independently what they need and when. It is like filling a tool box. We don't always need the hammer, but when we do it is nice to have it!

Literature Response Matrix

Retelling Box

BME Sheet

Tell a Tape

Create a Cover

The Little Red Hen

Four Flap Book

Buddy Reading

Write a Letter

Write Questions

Sketch a Scene

Make a Mobile

Find Fun Facts

Step Book

CHAPTER 5

Strategy Immersion in Centers

Tools That Target All Learners

Increase Time In Text

Choice Not Chaos

Keys to Success

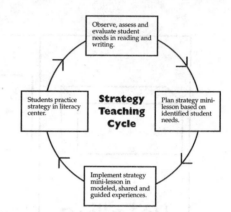

From Susan:

I remember the hours I spent making file folder games where kids matched nouns, verbs, contractions, and many other isolated skills. One of my first dates with my future husband was spent with him cutting out peas with words on them that were to be put in alphabetical order in their pods! Imagine my disappointment when I finally gave the pods to my third graders and they used the game for all of five minutes and announced, "I'm done! Now what do I do?" I wanted to answer, "I spent hours making that game! You will go back and play it again—and enjoy it!" So we were back at work the next night making a new game to keep the kids busy so I could teach small groups! This cycle is repeated in classrooms around the country everyday. Teachers are running themselves ragged trying to have enough stuff to keep kids busy so they can teach.

Kids learn to read by reading and write by writing. It sounds so simplistic that we often think we need to **do** more. *If I could just cover more... If I buy this new program... If I only spent more time on ...* Instead we miss the one thing we can truly give our students for relatively low cost: **more time immersed in text**. If you want to learn to snow ski, you need to practice. The more you practice, the

less you fall! We need to provide the same kind of intensive engaged practice with our students as they build their fluency within a variety of text. This can be done effectively within the context of literacy centers.

Centers sometimes become places where kids are expected to complete tasks that are meaningless and fragmented. The most effective centers are directly related to the instructional components of balanced literacy. When it is just busy work kids will lose interest quickly and centers will break down.

It is important for students to know and use a variety of the types of skills we put on those file folder games; however very few of the traditional language arts centers actually gave kids time to apply these skills in real reading and real writing situations. While not a focus in the past, today we know it is critical that our students have lots of practice within text to build their fluency. After all, the place we want them to use and apply skills and strategies is at the point of need within the context of their individual literacy experiences.

The goal of literacy centers is to provide students meaningful interactions with text. When we create meaning for our students, they begin to make connections between what is happening in the classroom and the application to their life-long literacy. It is a wonderful and amazing thing to watch the lightbulb click on for young learners. The first time you hear them announce, " I've seen that word before!" or "I've read a story like that one!" or "I can figure it out on my own!" you know they are developing their personal literacy in a meaningful way. They must be able to do this across a variety of text for many purposes.

Non-fiction Text

Traditionally, non-fiction text was withheld until a child knew how to read. Somewhere around the third grade we introduced science and social studies textbooks. Today, we know we must expose our students to a wide variety of genre at a very early age. It is ludicrous to think that children are not ready to handle informational text until they are eight years old or more. Even young children can learn to find information from the text around them. Walk into any Burger King with a two-year-old and tell them they are in McDonald's. They will set you straight very fast!

Kids develop understanding for informational text long before they ever get a sense of story. We need to nurture the young learner's inclination toward expository text. They love to learn about things that are true, especially if it is a real part of their world. Many educational publishers are now producing high interest non-fiction text for early grades. We must teach students how to read and comprehend this type of text.

For years teachers have been training students to handle informational text in much the same way they read and write literary text from cover to cover. This is an ineffective practice. Non-fiction text is not laid out in the same way. Non-fiction text has many entry points. Think about how you read a cookbook. Do you go from the first page straight through to the very last one? Usually you would flip through and glance at the pictures and the recipe titles. When you see something that appeals to you, you might stop and

read the text a little more carefully. The same is true with most non-fiction text. As Dr. Brenda Parkes says, "You dip into and out of non-fiction text."

You will see that many of our literacy centers require students to locate and extract information from informational text. In *Strategies That Work*, Stephanie Harvey and Anne Goudvis note, *Readers of non-fiction have to decide and remember what is important in texts they read if they are going to learn anything from them*. While this is a skill that begins to prepare them for upper grade testing, it is also one they will use over and over again as adults.

Spend time in shared and guided experiences that show students the features of non-fiction text. Demonstrate the application of these features in non-fiction text children find in their world such as menus, brochures, and newspapers. Provide opportunities for students to practice using these features to understand text in literacy centers. Some of the features of non-fiction text you will want to include in your mini-lesson instruction and center activities include:

Table of Contents - Why is it included? How can it help me read a book?

Bold Face Print - How can I find out what these words mean? Why did the author choose to write them in bold?

Charts and Diagrams - In what ways do these help me understand the text?

Picture Captions - When do I need to read any captions in text?

Index or Glossary - Why are these included? What does the author want me to know?

Integrating Non-fiction Text in Literacy Centers

There are many ways to get non-fiction text into the hands of your young learners during literacy center times. You will think of many on your own. Below is a list to get you started:

- **Classroom Library** - Clearly label baskets with non-fiction. Books can be sorted by title, author, or content. Keep a basket with past issues of your classroom news magazine (i.e. *Ranger Rick, Time for Kids, Scholastic News)* for students to re-visit.

- **Listening** - Have an older reader or parent volunteer record news articles from your classroom news magazine or your morning messages. Now your students can listen to the news.

- **Literature Response** - Teach children to create a WOW sheet after reading a non-fiction book, poem or article. Precut the capital letters in WOW on your school's die cut machine or handwrite them in bubble form. Attach these to a 6"x18" piece of construction paper. Students use markers to record two fact sentences from their book on each letter. Label the WOW sheet with the book title and have them share it with a friend.

    (Note: these are easier to read if children write each fact in a different color.)

- **Poetry** - Many poems are non-fiction. Write these on chart paper and illustrate (or let your children do it for you). Introduce the chart during shared reading. Talk about the information in the poem. What did you learn? Make small copies of the poem for children to include in their poetry notebook. (See page 120)

- **Research** - Fill this center with non-fiction books and magazines. Students can keep a log describing what they learn each time they read a new book or article. They should also be encouraged to generate questions about what they read. This will encourage further investigation into the topics represented in the book.

- **Word Work** - Fill your word work center with class-made and commercial dictionaries, thesaurus and other class-generated word reference charts. For young

children make a class list book similar to a phone book. Children will enjoy looking up and recreating their friends' names with magnetic letters.

- **Writing** - Keep a list of non-fiction writing suggestions posted in your writing center.

Write a letter

Make a list

Write directions

Write a recipe

Literary Text

Understanding literary texts and story elements comes from time spent reading and listening to the traditional bedtime story. This is often a part of the read aloud time in the early literacy classroom. Literary text differs from expository in that it shows a passage of time and includes story elements. Stories are designed to be read from beginning to end. For students to understand a story, they must be able to understand character, plot, setting and sequence of events.

Why do we expose children to quality literature in school? While we want to foster a love of language we want kids to become literate. To do this, we must put them into rich language experiences where they can read, re-read, speak, and write for authentic purposes. During a summer literacy workshop, I heard a presenter comment that he doesn't recall any of his students ever saying, "Can I go check out that worksheet at the library?" Kids who spend a lot of time in literary text begin to understand how it is constructed. They notice the author's craft and style. With enough exposure and encouragement, they will begin to try it out for themselves during their independent work.

Integrating Literary Text in Literacy Centers

We must be just as intentional about immersing students in literary text as we are in non-fiction text. Children need opportunities to experience, think about, and revisit a good story. Think about how many times you have heard a child request, "Read it again!" after you finished reading a much-loved book. Here are some ideas to get you started:

- **Classroom Library** - Label baskets and bookshelves by author, favorite characters, and other common fiction elements. Include a book recommendation chart in your book center. Ask your children to note which books they would recommend to a friend and why on a 3" x 5" sticky note. Post these on a chart labeled *Our Recommended Reading*.

- **Listening** - Provide several copies of a book along with its audiocassette. Purchase commercial storybooks on tape or ask your parents to donate some from home.

- **Literature Response** - Keep brown bags in this center for children to fill with small props or pictures to retell a story.

- **Poetry** - Write or type familiar nursery rhymes on $8^1/_2$" x 11" cardstock. Use clip art or children's drawings to illustrate and laminate them for durability. Your students will love reading and rereading these cards. Nursery Rhymes are a great start to Individual Poetry Notebooks in kindergarten and first grade. (See page 120).

- **Research** - Pair a fiction book with a non-fiction book about the same content. For example, *Rainbow Fish* by Marcus Pfister with an informational book about fish. Have students compare the two texts. Encourage them to think what the fiction author had to know to write their book.

- **Word Work** - Print up words from your favorite children's stories for students to sort. Provide book(s) at the center for students to reference.

- **Writing** - Older children will begin to write fantasy stories. Keep index cards with fictional character names, plots, settings, etc. to help stimulate student creativity.

Maintaining Text Balance

If we want children to have a wealth of experiences in listening to and understanding literature, we need to nurture understanding of both non-fiction and fiction text. We do this by providing rich experiences for our students in both genre such as those listed above.

Primary classrooms must be full of both fiction and non-fiction in a variety of forms: storybook, informational book, magazines, newspapers, poetry etc. Immersion in text builds stronger readers and writers. John David Cooper writes, *It is not the amount of activities which make better readers, it is the amount of reading.*

Kids begin to develop understanding of how text is arranged and how to handle different forms of text at different times. For example, if I hand a second grader a telephone book, he must understand that it is not intended to be read from beginning to end. The phone book has many entry points depending on what information needs to be accessed. Non-fiction text has many entry points. It is entirely possible for me to enter in the middle of an informational book and still glean information from my visit.

This depth of understanding only comes from spending time investigating the layout of informational text and contrasting that with the organization of story. If we want our students to understand this, we must put them to work investigating text in a variety of styles and genre. This exploration serves our students in the primary classroom, later on standardized testing, and well into their real life reading and writing experiences.

Classroom management expert, Harry Wong says, *The one who does all the work, is the one who learns.* I think back to those pea pods and I ask myself, "Who was doing the learning?" I want my students to not only be responsible for their learning, but to construct it through the support of the learning environment and the text I provide for them. Why? Well, one reason is that standardized tests are no longer multiple choice response. Testing is high stakes in most states now. While much of the testing begins in grade three and up, the early literacy teacher supplies an important piece of the testing puzzle.

Students must be able to read and write proficiently to succeed in our nation's schools. Teachers are being held accountable as never before. We cannot afford to lose a minute of valuable teaching and learning time. We all must see ourselves as third grade and fourth grade teachers! If we provide a solid foundation for our students, then upper-grade teachers will not be running ragged trying to make up lost ground.

The model no longer is book followed by worksheet, but book followed by book, or text followed by text. Students are being asked to compare and contrast, summarize, question, and infer from a variety of text and across genre. Therefore, the classroom must be filled with good literature, ample non-fiction text, as well as poetry, and environmental print. Students must have ample time to develop a comfort level with a wide variety of text. When they begin to build an understanding of the types of print out there, they will be able to maximize learning. Suddenly the text will not be a stumbling block, but a door for the child to move through as she digs for meaning and applies that meaning to her learning for that moment in time.

Creating a Meaningful Print Rich Environment

A critical part of immersion in text is creating a print rich environment. Many teachers just put print up without thinking what or why they are displaying it. The print in the classroom must be useful for more than filling space. It should be something kids will return to again and again for reference, to spark a new idea, and show off their accomplishments.

> **From Susan:**
>
> I remember the first time I heard about a print rich environment in a staff development workshop. I promptly returned to my classroom and labeled everything before the children returned the next day! Then I spent the rest of the year wondering why my students didn't appreciate all the work I did for them. When they needed to know how to spell a word often times it was right on the classroom wall. What had I done wrong? There is nothing wrong with labeling and installing print in the classroom, but the print I had hung up was only for me. It wasn't meaningful to my students.

Students must have ownership and input into the print that is displayed in the classroom. It must be directly related to the thinking and learning they are doing within the context of the balanced literacy framework.

From Mellissa:

I can still picture my first grade students looking for words on the word wall when they needed them. They put them there, so they knew where to look. I didn't hear "how do you spell _____" or "what do I do now?" quite as much. My students were in an environment that allowed them to locate information on their own.

When you fill your classroom with meaningful print and a wide range of text, you will be setting your students up for success as they work in centers. A self-assessment to help you decide if the print in your room is meaningful follows on page 42.

Is the print in my room meaningful?

	Yes	Somewhat	Not at All
Does the majority the print on my walls come from my literacy block? (i.e. reading and writing mini-lessons)			
Do my students have opportunities to interact with print on a daily basis both with me and by themselves?			
Does it include whole thoughts or ideas such as poem charts, language experience, or daily news?			
Are there plenty of books from a variety of genre neatly arranged and labeled clearly for student use?			
Are my students' names posted frequently in my room?			
Do I encourage the use of student names for letter study and print awareness?			
Is the print posted as a result of shared decision-making or is it mostly teacher-directed?			
Is student work posted and labeled to encourage students to revisit it from time to time?			
Does it include labels and directions for using tools and equipment in the classroom?			
Is it neat and easy to read?			
Are charts printed with alternating colors to aid young children in tracking print?			
Do I rotate the print frequently to encourage "freshness" in the classroom environment?			
Do I have places where students can go to find information without my help? (i.e. dictionaries, word walls, charts, etc)			
Do I revisit the print in my room from time to time to teach or reinforce skills and strategies?			

CHAPTER 6

Strategy Immersion in Centers

Tools That Target All Learners

Increase Time In Text

Choice Not Chaos

Keys to Success

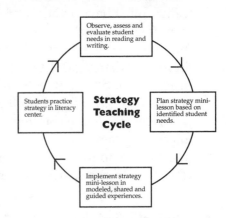

Strategy Teaching Cycle

Observe, assess and evaluate student needs in reading and writing.

Plan strategy mini-lesson based on identified student needs.

Implement strategy mini-lesson in modeled, shared and guided experiences.

Students practice strategy in literacy center.

Literacy centers should provide plenty of choices for students as they work, but they should not be chaotic. We want students to be engaged in their learning, so *you* can engage in teaching. Choice promotes engagement. Picture yourself walking into a nice steak restaurant and the waiter telling you, *I'm sorry, you can only have turkey tonight.* While you may love turkey, the minute someone suggests you can't have what you want or has taken your options away, you rebel and lose interest in the restaurant. The same is true of your students. We see many centers out there giving little choice or none at all. When we give kids choices, they have more ownership of their work and they often exceed our expectations of the kinds of learning and thinking we anticipate!

Giving choices supports individualism and allows for student preferences and interests within the classroom community. While there are times we need all kids to conform to a certain learning or response, choice builds engagement and engagement reduces chaos. Students must be able to demonstrate their ability to make wise choices in learning situations.

Implementing Choice

Choice is not always a let-freedom-reign-use-what-you-want-the-way-you-want type of thing. You can build choice into your centers

while still maintaining control over what is happening there. Following is a list of suggestions for implementing choice in your centers while avoiding chaos:

- **Students select from a variety of activities within a center**. For example at the writing center a student may choose to write in his writing folder, write the room (see page 179), or write on dry erase boards.

- **Students use a variety of materials to demonstrate understanding**. Every center must have a variety of materials to complete the work. Sometimes students find more authentic uses for the materials in centers than we do! One first grade teacher found her students creating games using word cards in the word work center. These children were manipulating language in a way that was meaningful to them at that point in time. This type of choice develops engagement in the learning environment.

- **Students work independently or collaboratively**. Students like to decide if and when they will work alone or in a group. The novelty of being able to write with a partner often moves the reluctant writer forward. We know that occasionally you need to see what a student can do on her own. In this case, you need to make your expectations clear to the student while letting her know that there will be other opportunities to work with a group.

- **Students choose ways to respond to a text.** When I read a good book, I do not always want to go out and make a diorama, write a letter to the main character, or write a new ending! Sometimes I just want to bask in the text with a friend. We must give our students some freedom in deciding how to respond to a text. We cannot always be so product-driven that our students lose the meat and meaning of their reading. The Literature Response Matrix described on page 35 is one way you can provide students choices in their responses to reading.

- **Students decide where to work in the classroom**. It is amazing what happens when you give kids a choice about where to work in the classroom. Sometimes just simply letting kids lay on the floor livens up a center activity and helps elevate the quality of work they produce.

Choice with Accountability

It's nice to have choices and some freedom, but you still must set the expectations of the kinds of thinking and learning that should be happening at each center. Teachers often ask us *How can I be sure that my students are learning while they are in centers?* They want to ensure student accountability for their time in centers. Since a large part of your centers will be open-ended process work, you will need to determine a system of checking. This can be as simple as a sign-in sheet posted in the center to a more complex learning log (See page 25). Both build responsibility for your students as they make choices within your centers.

Dealing with Chaos

We can hear you saying, *OK, I have provided choice and made my students accountable for work but my room is so chaotic during center time!* It's at this point that many teachers want to throw in the literacy center towel. Take a deep breath, step back and consider what it is that makes you uncomfortable. Is it the movement? Is it noise level? Is it misuse of materials? Whatever it is, decide what would make it better and come up with a solution **with** your students.

One first-grade teacher decided the movement and noise in her classroom was too much until she took time to focus on what was really happening in her classroom. She took a day off from small group instruction and observed her students' activity during center work. As usual, she was aware of a low hum in the room and plenty of movement. As she really focused in on the talk taking place, she found her students collaborating on work. She heard encouragement and learning take place from peer to peer. This was talk that, until that moment, she was unaware was happening. The movement, while excessive for one or two students, was mostly meaningful as students went to get supplies to complete their literacy center tasks. Once she understood the talk and movement was that of work and not off-task behavior, this teacher could go back to teaching small groups with confidence that the rest of her class was learning.

If you identify a problem, talk with your students and have them problem-solve with you. Discussing a problem and solution together will help ensure all students understand what is expected during center time. Holding a group meeting also gives students ownership in the processes of your classroom. When students have clear understanding of your expectations, they will be more confident in their roles during literacy centers.

CHAPTER 7

Strategy Immersion in Centers

Tools That Target All Learners

Increase Time In Text

Choice Not Chaos

Keys to Success

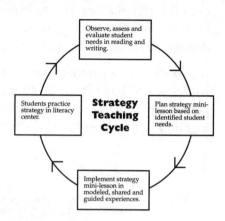

Questions and Answers

Should I expect products from students' work in centers?

We believe that it is OK to occasionally expect products from center activity. Teachers sometimes expect a product every time a student uses a center. Remember that the *process* is often the most important part of the center activity. Since students are going back into familiar texts, we recommend that you examine ways to collect products during your small- and whole-group-lessons.

How can I stay aware of my students' needs?

You must become a "kid watcher." This means that you must continually be observing, assessing and evaluating your students capabilities. When you know what they can do, then you can find ways to move them forward in their learning. When you know where they struggle, you can provide more support and in turn give them success with literacy tasks in the classroom.

What supports and challenges can I provide my students in the center setting?

When you become aware of your students' individual and group needs, you will be able to provide multilevel support for all of your students. Take time to watch students use a center you have set up in the classroom. Ask yourself if it is effective. If not, think about whether it needs to be easier or more difficult. You will not only be evaluating your students' performance in centers, but also your choice of centers for your students.

How can I stay aware of student performance in centers?

Take the time to walk around and observe their behavior. One second grade teacher walks around the classroom for five minutes between his guided reading groups. This allows him to see what his students are doing and redirect them as necessary. Use the Center Observation Record on page 48 to record responses to literature, ongoing tasks the student may be completing, or writing projects.

Why should I use heterogenous grouping for center time?

When you heterogeneously group you begin to build a community of learners. Students start to notice the strengths of their peers and rely on those to be successful in centers. You need to remain aware of social interaction as well as areas of need for your students when forming your groups. This will help you avoid conflicts that could arise.

How can I make sure that my centers are at an appropriate level of difficulty?

Review your students' center work and behavior to determine the effectiveness of center activities. We want to continue to challenge student learning, yet not force them to constantly be working at an inappropriate level of frustration. When you use the Center Observation Record on page 48 note the projects and assignments students are completing and their levels of difficulty.

How can I keep centers fresh for my students?

While most of your centers will not need to be changed frequently, you can keep them fresh and inviting simply by changing materials. It is amazing to watch what happens when you add a clipboard to the writing center or highlighters to the research center. Students enjoy using new medium such as paint or clay in the Literature Response Center. When you make these subtle changes it allows students to continue to practice and apply skills and strategies in new contexts.

Why do I need to use open-ended activities?

When you keep your center activities open-ended all students have the opportunity to work at their own level. Their responses may be the same format, but the text level will vary according to their individual reading and writing level.

Should I provide models for all projects and activities?

Many of your projects and activities will come from your reading or writing workshop lessons. Display any models you create for your mini-lessons in the appropriate center. Remind students that these are only models, and encourage them to use their own creativity and individuality when creating products and responses to literature.

How often should I model procedures and routines?

Although it sounds simple, the best answer we can give is *until they learn it.* Modeling and practicing procedures and routines for material use will help you establish a productive learning environment. Keep in mind you may have to model several times throughout the year. This should take place any time centers break down or you introduce new materials.

What do I do when centers "break down" or are ineffective?

Sometimes all you need to do is revisit the procedures and routines with your students. Observe what is happening in the center so you can discuss with your students the problem. Talk about possible solutions. Try them out and then revisit the problem to see if your solution is working.

Center Observation Record

Date	Student Name	Literature Response	Ongoing Task	Book Title	Poem Title	Notes

Literacy Connection Planners

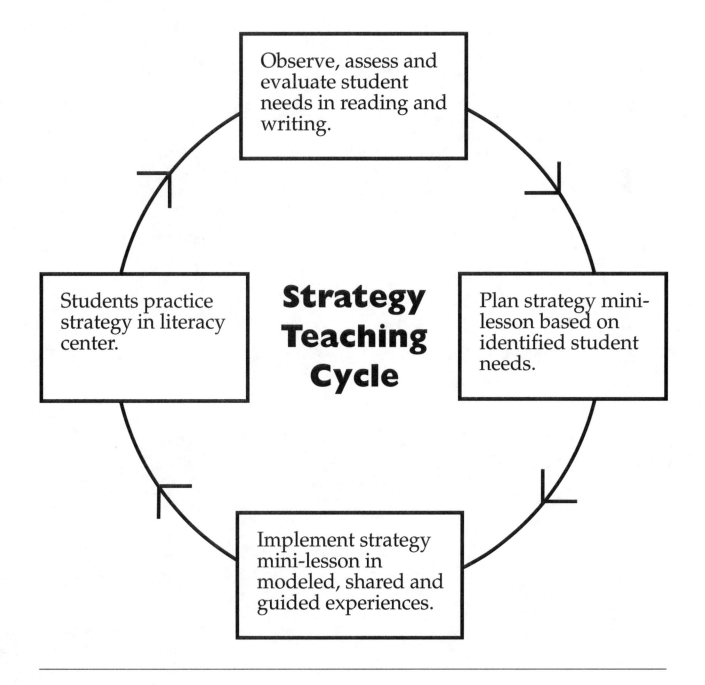

Observe, assess and evaluate student needs in reading and writing.

Students practice strategy in literacy center.

Strategy Teaching Cycle

Plan strategy mini-lesson based on identified student needs.

Implement strategy mini-lesson in modeled, shared and guided experiences.

Reading Connections

Strategies for Building Fluency and Independence - readers self-select appropriate text and read for a variety of purposes.

Page #	Mini-lesson Topic	Literacy Center Connection	Center Title
52	Using voice inflections when you read	Poetry	Poetry Pals
58	Building fluency in oral reading	Classroom Library	Read the Room
60	Self-selecting Text	Classroom Library	Book Pick of the Week
64	Retelling a story	Literature Response	Act It Out!

Literacy Connection Planner
Using Voice Inflections When You Read

Reading Strategy: Strategies for Building Fluency and Independence

Materials:
____ *Yo! Yes?* by Chris Raschka
____ Poetry Pals Procedures chart for Poetry Center
____ Playback Pipe (You can use an elbow PVC pipe for students to read into. This helps them hear themselves as an audience would.)
____ Poetry Pals Discussion Log

Mini-lesson:

Readers' Workshop Component: Interactive Read Aloud

1. Begin by reading aloud the book *Yo! Yes?* by Chris Raschka with no voice inflection. After reading a couple of pages, stop and ask the students if they notice something different about this read aloud.

2. Discuss with them the importance of reading the punctuation to build meaning. Demonstrate by reading the title again using the punctuation.

3. Read the book through with fluency, voice inflections and expression. Talk with the students about how this changes the way they understand the story.

4. Re-read the text. Invite your students to join in by reading for one of the characters.

5. Remind students of the importance of using voice inflections during reading to help the reader understand.

6. One of the best ways to express fluency and voice inflections is when reading poetry. Explain to the students that they will have the opportunity to take part in Poetry Pals where they will learn to read and perform a poem with fluency and expression.

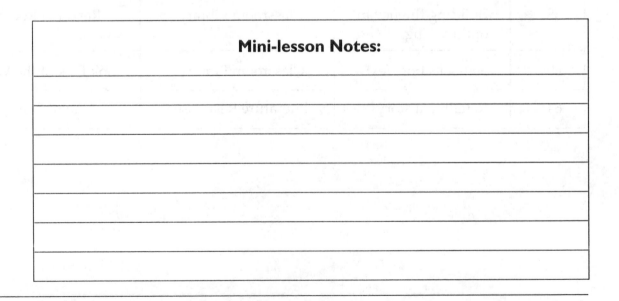

Mini-lesson Notes:

Literacy Center Connection:

Poetry Center: Poetry Pals

Place a variety of familiar and unfamiliar poems in your poetry center. These can be on chart paper, overhead transparencies, books, file folders etc. Assign each student to a Poetry Pals group. This could be the group who will be at the Poetry Center at the same time. Each **student** will do the following.

1. Choose a poem.

2. Rehearse the poem until you feel you know it well.

3. Read it into the playback pipe to listen to how the audience will heara you.

4. Try it with a new rhythm, read it to music, or use a new voice.

5. When it sounds just right to you, read it to two of your Poetry pals group members.

6. Ask for group member feedback.

7. Fill out one of the Poetry Pals Response Logs (pages 55-56) and discuss in your group.

Lesson Variation and Notes:

- You can monitor group discussions using a tape recorder. This will provide feedback on your students' learning and interactions during their group sessions.

- Display familiar poems from the shared reading experience throughout the classroom for students to practice reading in the poetry center.

- Students can keep a log of the poems they have learned and shared in their group. (See page 57)

- Help kids tune their ears to language and fluency by putting poems and poetry books in your listening center.

- Occasionally record your students reading a familiar poem on a tape. Put these tapes in your listening center with a copy of the text.

Poetry Pals Procedures

1. Choose a poem to read.

2. Use your body and your voice to read it.

3. Read it with rhythm.

4. Practice it until you know it.

5. Read it into the play back pipe.

6. Read your poem to a friend.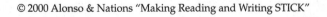

Poetry Pals Response Log

Name _____ Title of Poem _____

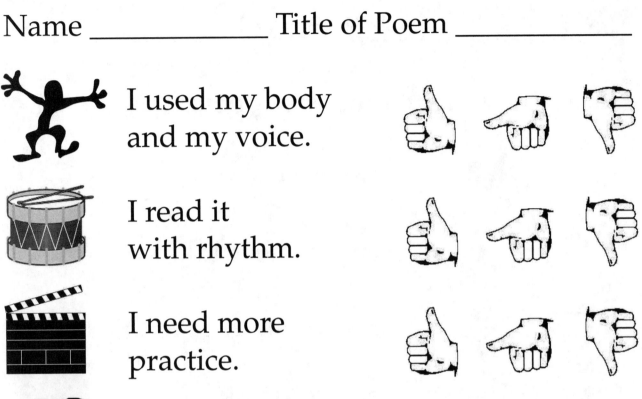

I used my body and my voice.

I read it with rhythm.

I need more practice.

The person who listened to me was:

_____

My thoughts: _____

_____

_____

_____

_____

Poetry Pals Response Log

Name _____ Poem Title _____

Here's how I feel about my poem:

☐ ♥   I loved it!

☐ 💡   It made me think.

☐ 👥   I plan to share it with a friend.

☐ 👎   I didn't like it.

Here's how I think I read my poem:

☐ 🕺   I used my body and my voice.

☐ 🥁   I kept the rhythm.

☐ 🎬   I need more practice.

Discuss your answers with your Poetry Pals Group.

_____'s Poetry Log

Date	Name of Poem and Author	Date Shared

Literacy Connection Planner
Building Fluency in Oral Reading

Reading Strategy: Strategies for Building Fluency and Independence

Materials: ____ Poems and charts displayed around the room.
____ Pointers
____ Eyeglass frames without lenses (Available from the local vision care center)

Mini-lesson:

Readers' Workshop Component: Shared Reading

1. Begin by thinking aloud:

   Good readers always want to get better at reading. One way to get better at reading is to practice reading over and over. When I plan to read you a book, I always read it several times before I read it to you. I do this so I can think about how it should be read and what my voice should sound like. This helps me to practice so I can read it without messing up. Today we are going to practice one of our old favorites to learn and to get better at reading.

2. Select a pointer and read with your students a few times. (Note: Pre-select familiar text so your students are past the word identification stage and ready to move to oral fluency.) Discuss ways to read with meaning and emotion during this practice time.

3. After reading the poem or chart two or three times, split your class into groups of three or four and let them practice reading small copies of the poem to each other. Talk about the difference that practice makes.

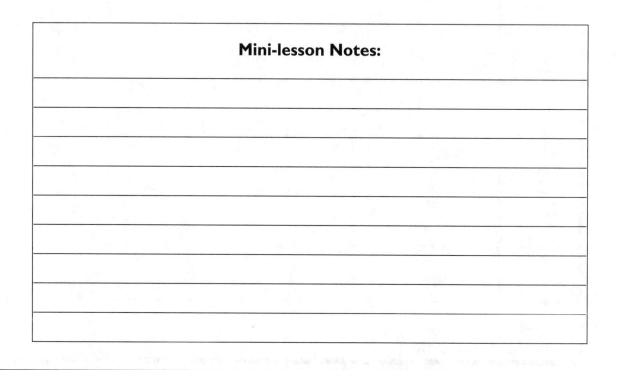

Mini-lesson Notes:

Literacy Center Connection:

Classroom Library: Read the Room

Store several pointers in a can in your classroom library labeled *Read the Room*. Two students at a time may choose a pointer and read the poems and charts displayed around your room. Include "reading glasses" (frames with the lenses removed) for even more fun!

Lesson Variation and Notes:

- Some things that can be used for pointers include:

  batons
  paint sticks decorated by you and your students
  rulers
  pencils with fun erasers
  toy light sabers
  flashlights
  back scratchers
  fly swatters

- Many of these items can be purchased at your local discount store.

- Remember to teach your students proper use of pointers. Consider limiting Reading the Room to two or three students to minimize inappropriate pointer use.

- Some poetry books we suggest:

  Poetry Place Anthology compiled and published by Scholastic, Inc.
  A Poem a Day by Helen More
  Animal Poems From A to Z by Meish Goldish

Literacy Connection Planner
Self-selecting Text

Reading Strategy: Strategies to Build Fluency and Independence

Materials: ____ A book that was recommended to you by a friend
____ A book that you are recommending for your students
____ Book Pick of the Week Poster (see page 62)

Mini-lesson:

Readers' Workshop Component: Read Aloud

1. Begin by sharing with students the following think-aloud:

   Sometimes when I want to pick out a book to read, I think about what my friends have recommended.

2. If possible, share a real experience you have had where a friend has recommended a book to you. Example: *My friend Mellissa called me the other night and told me about the book, <u>Twilight Comes Twice</u> by Ralph Fletcher. I immediately went out to the bookstore to look for the book. When I looked at it, I knew it was one I would like to have in my personal library.*

3. Talk about times when students have heard about a book from a friend or family member.

4. Say, *We are going to begin a Book Pick of the Week in our Library Center. I will begin by posting one of my recommended books. Then as the weeks go on, you can post your own recommendations in the center. We can all check out the poster to see if there is a book we would like to read.*

5. Choose a book to post. Designate a day where the book pick of the week will be your read aloud.

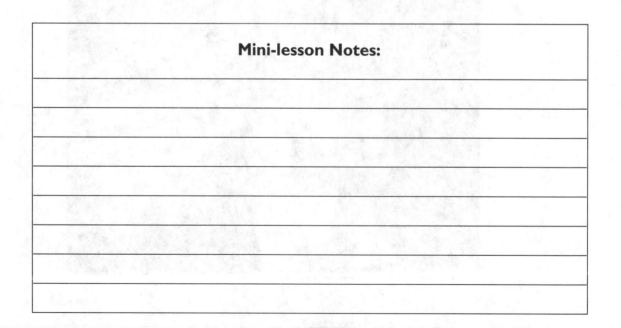

Mini-lesson Notes:

Literacy Center Connection:

Library Center: Book Pick of the Week

Create a poster for your book center like this:

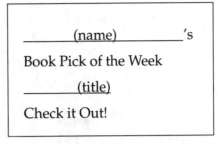

_____(name)_____'s

Book Pick of the Week

_____(title)

Check it Out!

Keep the Book Pick of the Week available for students to browse during sustained silent reading and centers. Designate a day of the week when you will read aloud the Book Pick of the Week. Rotate the weeks among your children. This may become so popular you will have to have two or three posters!

Lesson Variations and Notes:

- Another fun way for students to begin recommending books to each other is through book talks. Allow students one minute to talk to the class about their books. They should tell what they liked about the books and why they recommend others read them.

- Your students can draw cartoon advertisements recommending books to read. Post these in your classroom library.

- Provide a sign-up chart for students to alert you they have a book recommendation to share. This allows you to monitor what is going up on the chart. Older students may like to apply to be able to post their book using the form on page 63.

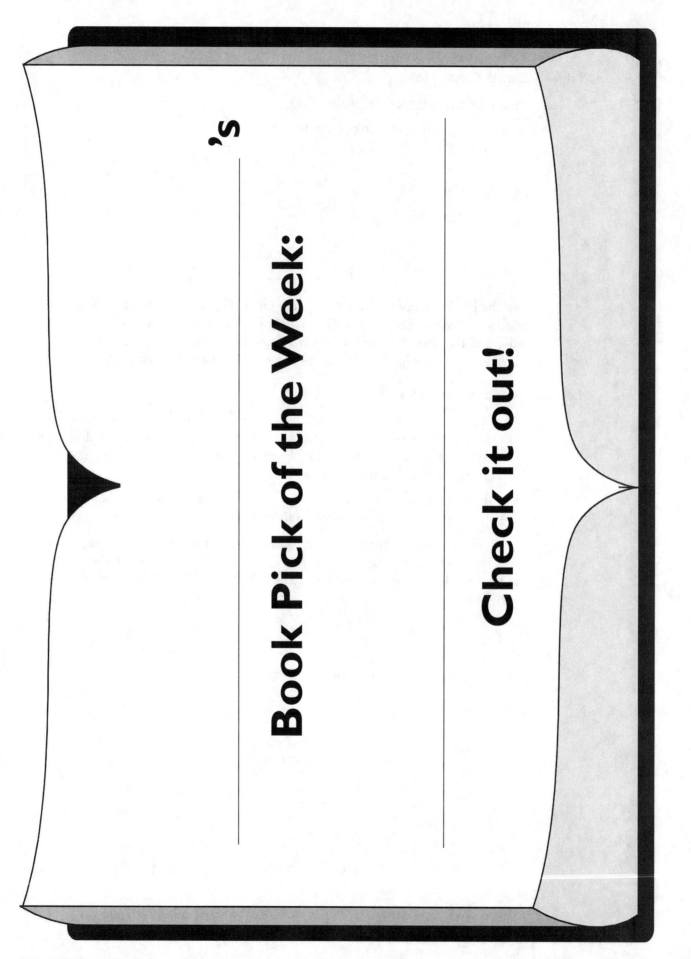

's

Book Pick of the Week:

Check it out!

Book Pick of the Week — Application Forms

I'd like to make the Book Pick of the Week.

Name: _____ Date: _____

Title: _____

Author: _____

Why I want to recommend this book: _____

_____

_____

I'd like to make the Book Pick of the Week.

Name: _____ Date: _____

Title: _____

Author: _____

Why I want to recommend this book: _____

_____

_____

I'd like to make the Book Pick of the Week.

Name: _____ Date: _____

Title: _____

Author: _____

Why I want to recommend this book: _____

_____

_____

Literacy Connection Planner
Retelling a Story

Reading Strategy: Strategies for Building Fluency and Independence

Materials: ____ Text from your read aloud and shared reading experiences
____ A Prop Box (see page 67 for example)

Mini-lesson:

Readers' Workshop Component: Read Aloud

1. Choose a book you have read before. Pre-select items to start your story-telling box. These items should be necessary to retell the book you are going to read.

2. Before reading ask your students to talk about what they remember about the book. *What happened in the beginning? The middle? The end?*

3. After several students have responded, read the book. Tell the students you want them to listen for important details. Those things which make this story special.

4. When you are finished reading talk about what the students think would be important to tell this story to somebody who has never seen the book. Record responses on chart paper.

5. Show the students the prop box you have assembled. Ask them to identify how many items you have in your box that could help in telling or acting out the important details listed on the chart.

6. Select several students to help retell the story using the props provided.

Mini-lesson Notes:

Literacy Center Connection:

Literature Response/Library: Act it Out!

Keep a prop box in this center stocked with items for retelling familiar stories. Encourage students to work together to retell the story. Periodically change items in the box to keep it fresh for your students. Provide plenty of pens, pencils, markers and paper for students who decide to write their own play about a book they have read.

Lesson Variations and Notes:

- We suggest you gather prop box materials at yard sales and thrift stores. There are many things you will find that will become treasured pieces to add to your prop boxes.

- Classroom parents provide a source for prop box materials. They often have "just what you're looking for"; they just don't know it! Send home a letter like the one below asking your parents to be an extra set of eyes for you.

Dear Parents,

One very important part of learning to read is being able to retell stories in our own words. This year we will practice retelling in many ways. One fun way for kids to practice this important skill is by creating plays to re-enact the story.

I am in the process of creating several prop boxes to help children with their retellings. I am attaching a list of items we could use in our prop boxes. If you have access to any of these items and would be willing to donate them, please let me know.

Thanks for your help in making our classroom an exciting place to learn and grow!

Sincerely,

Retelling Planner

Group Members: _____

_____

_____

Book Title: _____

Author: _____

Important Characters: _____

_____

_____

Important Part(s): _____

_____

_____

Props We Will Need: _____

_____

_____

What We Will Say:

Prop Box Ideas for Some Familiar Children's Books and Nursery Rhymes

Goldilocks and The Three Bears
3 bowls (varying sizes)
3 blankets or towels (for beds)
A cereal box
Apron

Little Red Riding Hood
Red ball cap
Basket
Empty muffin box
A blanket for grandma's bed
Wolf ears (made out of pipe cleaners and felt)

Little Boy Blue
Blue cap or cape
Toy horn
Yellow blanket or towel for haystack
Plastic corn

The Three Pigs
Some straw (cut up yellow construction paper)
Some sticks
A brick (Use a piece of foam or a block)
Soup spoon

If You Give a Mouse a Cookie
Cardboard cookie cut from brown posterboard
Empty glue bottle
Crayons
Cup

Little Miss Muffett
Small stool
Bowl and spoon
Plastic spider

Reading Connections

Strategies for Comprehension - readers construct meaning from a variety of text.

Page #	Mini-lesson Topic	Literacy Center Connection	Center Title
70	Revisiting text for deeper understanding	Research Center	Fact Sort
78	Predicting	Classroom Library	I Predict...
80	Making personal connections in my reading	Literature Response	Connection Collection
84	Thinking about and responding to text	Literature Response	In My Book

Literacy Connection Planner
Revisiting Text for Deeper Understanding

Reading Strategy - Strategies for Comprehension

Materials:
_____ *Stellaluna* by Janell Cannon
_____ Removable highlighter tape (2 colors)
_____ Large T-chart on chart paper
_____ Small Bats/Birds T-chart (see page 73 for reproducible T-chart)
_____ *Stellaluna* fact Sort Cards (see pages 74 and 75 for *Stellaluna* fact sort cards)

Mini-lesson:

Readers' Workshop Component: Read Aloud

1. Read and discuss the book *Stellaluna* by Janell Cannon. (This may be done a day prior to this mini-lesson.)

2. Revisit *Stellaluna* with a think aloud such as:

   When I read a book, sometimes I think the author is trying to teach me something. When I go back to the book Stellaluna I think Janell Cannon wants me to notice the difference between bats and birds. This will help me understand the book better. I don't always remember what I have read, so I have to go back and reread parts of the text. Let's do that together.

3. Go back into *Stellaluna* and locate places where the author describes bat behavior and bird behavior. Use one color of removable highlighting tape to highlight specific details about bat behavior in the text. For example, *I'm a bat. I am hanging by my feet.* Use the second color to highlight specific details about bird behavior. *She slept in the nest at night.*

4. Record these details on a T-chart labeled *Bats/Birds*.

5. Summarize this lesson by reminding students of the importance of revisiting text:

   I think Janell Cannon wanted us to understand the difference between bats and birds so we could understand why Stellaluna couldn't live like a bird.

6. Discuss with your students how this knowledge helps them understand the story better and how revisiting text is a way to build deeper understanding when they read.

Mini-lesson Notes:

Literacy Center Connection:

Research Center: Fact Sort

Place a copy of the book *Stellaluna* in the Research Center along with the small T-chart labeled "Bats/Birds." Duplicate *Stellaluna* fact Sort Cards. For added durability, attach the cards to tagboard strips and laminate prior to cutting them apart. Have students go back into the text to sort the facts on the T-chart. For additional support, keep the highlighting tape from your mini-lesson in the book labeling each fact.

Storage Tip: Store all sort cards in a small sandwich bag. Use velcro to stick the bag inside the back cover of the book.

Lesson Variations and Notes:

- Duplicate the sorting pages for each student to cut and glue facts to an individual chart for use as a record of their center activity.

- Provide other texts on bats and birds. Let students add some of their own facts to the class t-chart.

- Place other informational story books in the center for students to create other fact charts.

- Have students create a learning log to record what they learned from the text and share it with a friend.

- Use fiction text to model revisiting text to understand character, setting, dialogue exchanges, plot descriptive language etc.

- Use the blank sort cards and t-chart on pages 76-77 to create other sorting opportunities for your students.

Stellaluna
by Janell Cannon

1. Read the book <u>Stellaluna</u> and the fact cards.

2. Use the highlighting tape to find the facts in the book.

3. Decide if the fact is about bats or birds.

4. Sort the cards on the t-chart labeled, "Bats/Birds."

5. Share your sort with a friend.

Stellaluna T-Chart

bats | birds

Stellaluna Sort Cards

Has thumbs.	Can see at night.
Cannot see at night.	Can carry its baby when it flies.
Lands on its feet.	Does not land on its feet.
Owls are its predator.	Learns to fly by mother pushing it from the nest.

Stellaluna Sort Cards

Sleeps at night.	Uses its sense of smell to find ripe fruit.
Feeds its babies bugs and crawly things.	Stays awake in the day.
Stays awake in the night.	Sleeps during the daytime.
Sleeps hanging by its feet.	Sleeps in a nest.

Blank T-Chart

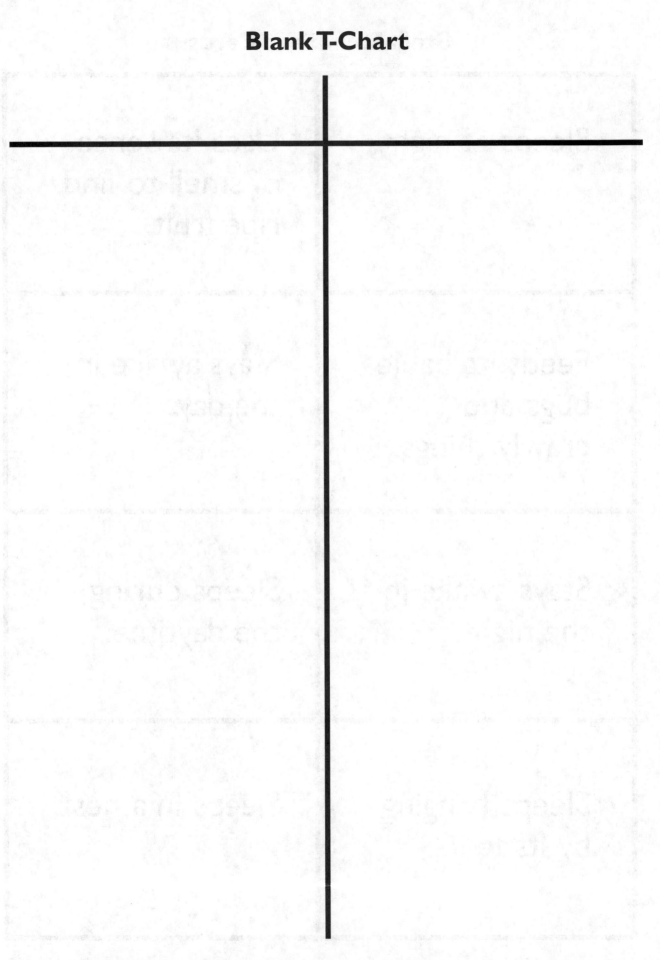

Blank Sort Cards

Literacy Connection Planner
Predicting

Reading Strategy: Strategies for Comprehension

Materials: ____ Read-aloud books
____ Post-it notes (3" x 5")
____ Gallon size storage bag

Mini-lesson:

Readers' Workshop Component: Read Aloud

1. Think aloud: *When I get ready to read a book I look at many things. Sometimes I look at the pictures on the cover and ask myself if it is a book I would like. Other times I look at the title and think about what might be inside the book. Good readers are always predicting what the book will be about. If I pick up a recipe book I would not expect there to be information about frogs. My predicting tells me that I will probably read about food and cooking.*

2. Introduce the new read aloud with the title covered. Ask students to use the information they have to make a prediction. What clues do they have to predict a title?

3. Elicit and discuss your students' predictions. Talk about how their predictions help them understand the book better.

4. Explain that they will have the opportunity to make predictions during center time about books you will be reading aloud in the future.

5. Each week post a new book for title predictions. Continue to ask students how their predictions help them understand the book.

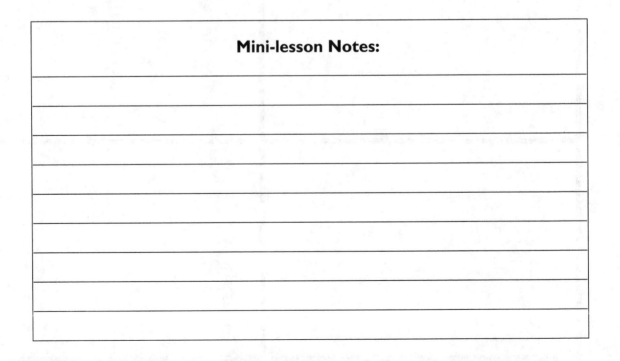

Mini-lesson Notes:

Literacy Center Connection:

Classroom Library: I Predict. . .

1. Cover the title of a book you are planning to read-aloud with sticky notes.

2. Secure the book in a gallon-size zipper bag and attach to a bulletin board.

3. Provide slips of paper for students to record their title predictions.

4. Post these on the bulletin board near the book.

5. Share and discuss the predictions before you reveal the book title.

Lesson Variations and Notes:

- Young children will enjoy using the title to predict the cover.

- Sort and classify predictions. Help students to see how their thinking is like their peers.

- Have your students make predictions before they read a new book during independent reading time.

- Suzi Boyett, second grade teacher, posts the "I Predict" in her classroom library with sticky notes for students to record and post their predictions.

Literacy Connection Planner
Making Personal Connections in My Reading

Reading Strategy: Strategies for Comprehension

Materials:
_____ *The Relatives Came* by Cynthia Rylant
_____ A variety of read aloud books
_____ Connection Collection Poster
_____ Paper
_____ Pre-cut squares, circles and hands (optional)
_____ Writing and drawing tools

Mini-lesson:

Readers' Workshop Component: Read Aloud

1. Read and discuss the book *The Relatives Came* by Cynthia Rylant.

2. Explain text-to-self connection: *Sometimes when I read a book it makes me think about something I have seen or done, someone I know, or somewhere I have been. When this happens, I am connecting to the book. We call this a text-to-self connection.*

3. Make sure your students understand the idea of personal connections then demonstrate by making a personal connection with the book. For example, *When I read the book The Relatives Came and I get to the part where she describes all the extra breathing in the house it makes me think about visiting my grandparents home as a child. Boy did my grandfather snore! I remember at night when we would all go to sleep it seemed like you could hear him breathing and whistling all over the house!*

4. This experience helps me understand what Cynthia Rylant meant when she wrote the part about all the extra breathing in the house.

5. Ask students to share their own personal connections with the group.

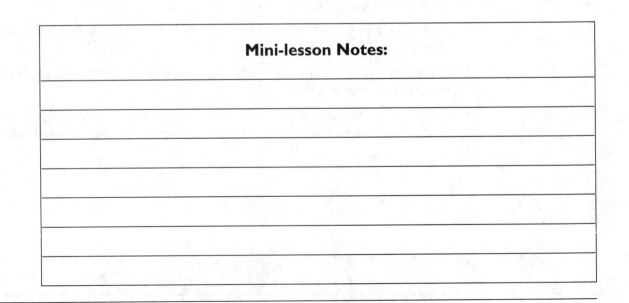

Mini-lesson Notes:

Literacy Center Connection:

Literature Response: Connection Collection

Invite students to begin keeping a Connection Collection Log. You can make a log for each child by stapling several pieces of newsprint together. They can write or draw a picture showing the personal connections they make in books they read or hear. Occasionally invite them to share connections from their logs during class meetings.

Lesson Variations and Notes:

- Text-to-Self, Text-to-Text, and Text-to-World is based on the work of Ellin Keene and Susan Zimmerman from their book, *Mosaic of Thought* (Heinemann).

- Gradually add Text-to-Text and Text-to-World after your students are comfortable with text-to-self.

- Remind your students to tell you how their connection helps them understand the book better.

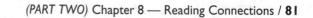

Connection Collection

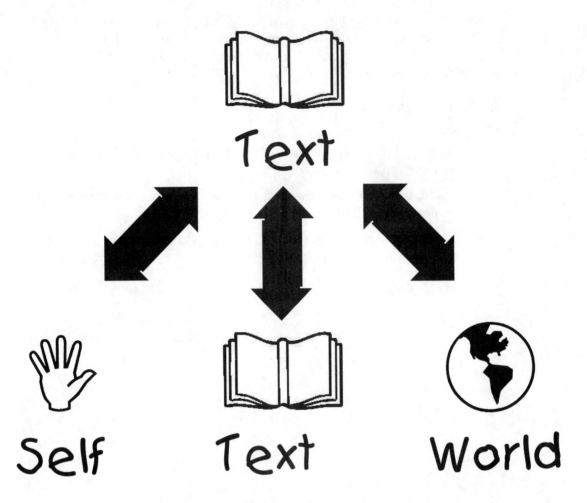

Text

Self **Text** **World**

What connection did you make?
Use the symbols to add your
connection to your log. Don't forget
to write the title!

Based on <u>Mosaic of Thought</u> by Keene and Zimmerman

Text

World

My Connection Collection Log

Name: _____

Self

Literacy Connection Planner
Thinking About and Responding to Text

Reading Strategy: Strategies for Comprehension

Materials: ____ Shared reading books (fiction and non-fiction)
____ Reading Response Sentence Stem Chart
____ Paper
____ Writing tools

Mini-lesson:

Readers' Workshop Component: Shared Reading

1. Pull out several familiar shared reading books. Ask your students to tell you what they remember about some of them.

2. Discuss what kinds of things we remember when we read books: characters, what we like, how we feel, things we notice, etc.

3. Think aloud: *When good readers read books they think about what they are reading. In their mind they make notes about what they notice, what they think, or how they feel. Thinking about my reading helps me understand what I read. When I notice something in the book that I think is interesting, it seems to stick in my mind.*

4. Share a book with the whole class.

5. Post the sentence stem "I notice..." in a pocket chart.

6. Invite your students to write or draw a response to the stem. Remind them to put the title and author on their response sheet.

7. Post these in the pocket chart with the stem "I notice.."

8. Encourage students to use the stem to respond to independent reading.

Mini-lesson Notes:

Literacy Center Connection:

Literature Response: Reading Responses

Post the sentence stem "I notice. . ." on a chart in your Literature Response center. Provide plenty of paper, pencils, and markers for students to write and illustrate their response. Gradually add the other stems to the chart. Students can use the chart as a reference anytime they want to write a response to their reading.

Lesson Variations and Notes:

- Students can record their reading responses in a spiral bound notebook.

- Occasionally respond to your students' writing. You might write *I did not notice _____ in this book, but I did notice _____. Did you like the part about _____?* Or *Why do you think the author chose _____?*

In my book....

👁 I notice...

💡 I think...

♥ I like...

✓ I learned...

❓ I wonder...

Reading Connections

Strategies for Finding Information - readers gather, evaluate, and synthesize data from a variety of sources.

Page #	Mini-lesson Topic	Literacy Center Connection	Center Title
88	Locating information in text	Research	Attraction Action
92	Generating questions before, during and after reading	Research	Question Collection
98	Locating information in the classroom environment	Classroom Library	How to Use this Room!
102	Using features of non-fiction text to find information	Classroom Library	Find the Feature

Literacy Connection Planner
Locating Information in Text

Reading Strategy: Strategies for Finding Information

Materials: ____ Attraction or travel brochures (available in hotel lobbies or from AAA)

____ Question Cards Template (page 91)

Mini-lesson:

Readers' Workshop Component: Shared Reading

1. Give each student an attraction brochure. Ask each to take a few minutes to share with a partner the things they notice in the brochure.

2. Explain that these brochures are full of information about the attraction. Ask students to read language that tells about their attractions.

3. Draw attention to informational pieces such as maps, price lists, dates and times of different events, etc. Talk about how these help the reader decide whether or not to visit that attraction.

4. Use a sample set of questions to model how to look for information in a brochure. Show your students how to look for headings where they might find the information to answer the question.

5. Complete one set of questions together to model recording the information.

6. Share with students that they will be able to complete Attraction Action when they visit the Research Center.

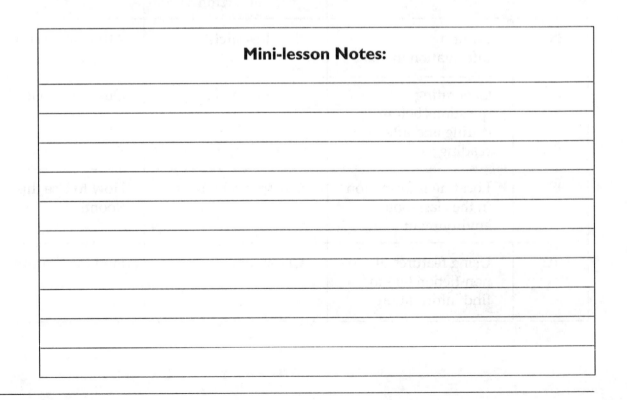

Mini-lesson Notes:

Literacy Center Connection:

Research: Attraction Action

Fill a shoebox with a variety of attraction brochures for your students to research. You can create questions that are specific to the individual attraction or leave your questions general to encourage students to read and research a variety of attraction brochures. We have provided a set of generic questions on page 90. For younger children, use a second brochure to cut picture clues to place on question cards. This will help students be able to locate the information easier.

Refresh this center by adding new brochures and questions periodically. This will keep students interested and encourage them to revisit this source of non-fiction text again.

Storage Tip: When you create specific questions for a brochure, hole punch the brochure and attraction cards and attach them with a key ring.

Lesson Variation and Notes:

- You can color-code or label questions in order of difficulty to meet the different levels in your classroom. You might simply label them: Easy, A Little Harder, Challenging. You may find that some students pick questions that are too easy or too challenging for their independent learning level. You can guide them to the questions you would like to see them try when you help them plan their literacy center time.

- Have students write or call visitors bureaus from other states to request information packets. Use these packets and brochures to have students research the area and report their findings with the rest of the class.

- Students can create their own brochures for a state or area they choose to research.

- Reinforce problem-solving and mathematical skills by using numerical information on the brochure to create word problems and investigations.

Question Cards

1. Name your attraction. Tell where it is located.

2. Why would someone want to visit this attraction? Use details from the brochure to explain your answer.

3. List three things you could see while visiting this attraction.

4. How can I find out more information about this place?

5. Are there directions on the brochure? How would I get to the attraction from our school?

6. How much would it cost a family of 4 to visit the attraction? If there is no price list, how can you find out?

7. Are there places for visitors to eat? Tell where you would eat lunch and why.

8. How long would you need to stay to see the entire attraction? Use details from the brochure to explain your answer.

Question Cards

Literacy Connection Planner
Generating Questions Before, During and After Reading

Reading Strategy: Strategies for Finding Information

Materials: _____ Laminated picture cards (photographs, magazines, newspapers)
_____ Shared reading text (non-fiction)
_____ Chart paper and markers (or Overhead Transparency of page 94)
_____ Highlighting tape or Wikki Sticks
_____ Question Collection Chart (page 95)

Mini-Lesson:

Readers' Workshop Component: Shared Reading/Shared Writing

1. Select a non-fiction text for shared reading and discuss the importance of asking questions **before, during and after reading** to find information about a topic.

2. Think aloud as you model asking questions **Before** the reading: *When I chose this book, I looked carefully at the cover photograph. I noticed there was a picture of a butterfly resting on a flower. It made me think of several questions about butterflies. I want to know: why is the butterfly sitting on this flower? How can a caterpillar change into a butterfly? How long does a butterfly live? I am going to write these questions on our chart under the section titled **Before**. These are questions I have even before I start to read.* Record your questions and add any the students ask.

3. Begin reading the text. Have students generate questions about the topic as you read. Record these questions on the chart under the heading **During**.

4. Continue to model the questioning process and have students generate questions they have when you finish the text. Record these questions on the chart under the heading **After** the reading.

5. Explain that these **After** questions could be used to launch a research investigation. Discuss sources students could use to search other books for the answers to their questions.

6. Return to the question chart. Use markers, Wikki Sticks or highlighting tape to emphasize the question stems used at the beginning of each question. Record these on a separate chart to keep at the center. This will provide support to students who may later need it.

Mini-lesson Notes:

Literacy Center Connection:

Research: Question Collection

Share with students they will be practicing how to collect questions at the Research Center. Model how to select a picture card and record questions on the Question Collection sheet.

Stock the Research Center with a picture card collection. You can start your collection using photographs, magazine or newspaper pictures and gluing them to a sheet of construction paper. Laminate for extra durability. Place the Question Collection handout at the center to serve as recording sheets for students. After your students have had plenty of practice generating questions with pictures add short articles or books to the center. Use the Question Collection recording sheet on page 97 to have them identify their questions. They should circle when the question occurred: before, during or after their reading.

Storage Tip: Here are a few suggestions for organizing the picture card collection.

- Place pictures in a file box and organize by theme, title, etc.

- Keep pictures in a three-ring binder and separate into page protectors.

- Remember to laminate pictures for durability.

Lesson Variation and Notes:

- For younger students, model the lesson above by using a picture card to generate questions instead of books. Older readers will begin to apply this strategy to their reading with on-going modeling and practice.

- Place the *Before , During, and After* charts at the Research Center as students move to independent reading of non-fiction text.

- Record question stems on sentence strips and place in a pocket chart at the center for support (Why does…, How can…, etc)

Our Questions About:

_____

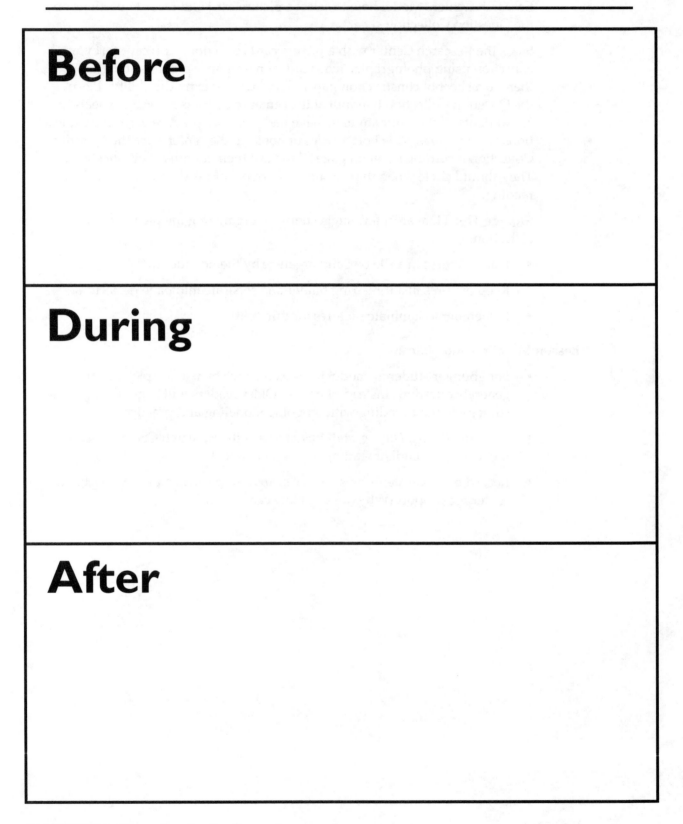

Before

During

After

Question Stems

Who will?

What did?

Where is?

When can?

Why will?

How did?

Who can?

What is?

Where did?

When is?

How will?

Who will?

What is?

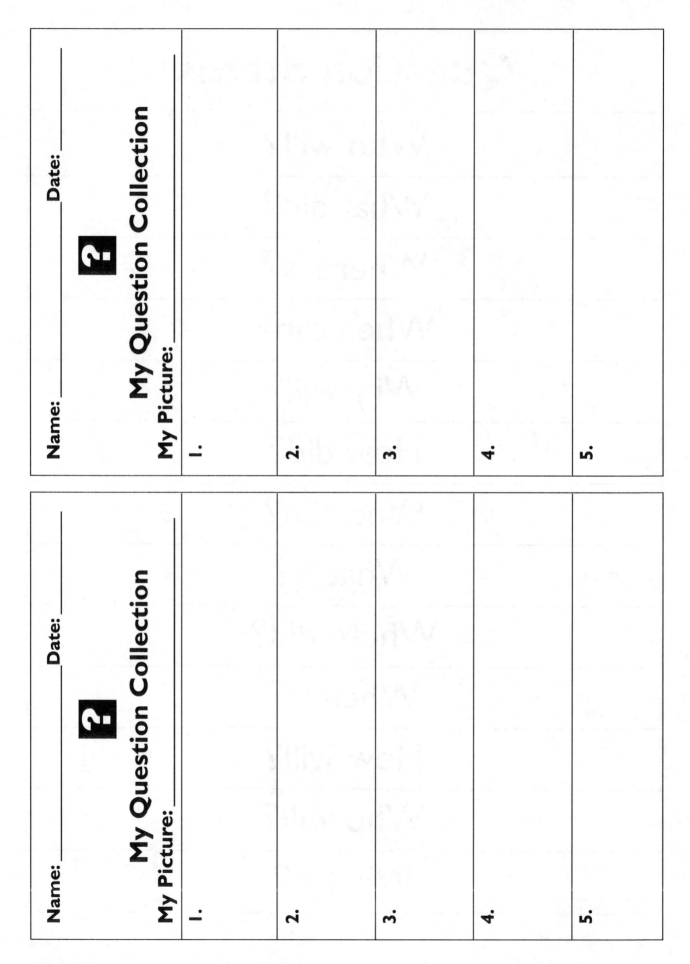

Name: _____ **Date:** _____

? **My Question Collection**

My Picture: _____

1.

2.

3.

4.

5.

Name: _____ **Date:** _____

? **My Question Collection**

My Picture: _____

1.

2.

3.

4.

5.

Name: _____ **Date:** _____

(Circle when the question occurred: before,
during or after your reding) **?**

My Question Collection

My Book: _____

1.

                            Before During After

2.

                            Before During After

3.

                            Before During After

4.

                            Before During After

5.

                            Before During After

Name: _____ **Date:** _____

(Circle when the question occurred: before,
during or after your reding) **?**

My Question Collection

My Book: _____

1.

                            Before During After

2.

                            Before During After

3.

                            Before During After

4.

                            Before During After

5.

                            Before During After

Literacy Connection Planner
Locating Information Within the Classroom Environment

Reading Strategy: Strategies for Finding Information

Materials: _____ Sentence strips or scavenger hunt (page 100)
_____ Your classroom
_____ Chart paper
_____ Markers

Mini-lesson:

Readers' Workshop Component: Shared Writing

1. Have students identify places in the classroom that give them information. Record these ideas on chart paper. Examples may include:

   - Calendar
   - Word Wall
   - Birthday Graph
   - Classroom Library
   - Research Center
   - Job Charts
   - Bulletin Boards
   - Class News

2. Divide the class into partners. Give each pair a sentence strip with a question such as, *Where could I go to find out who is a bus rider?* Have the pairs physically go to the place that would give them the answer to the question. Trade sentence strips and continue to try to answer the questions by standing next to the source of information within the classroom.

3. During a follow-up lesson, model how to write a short description of each of these areas in the classroom. Have students help write the description for each area. Turn these descriptions into a big book.

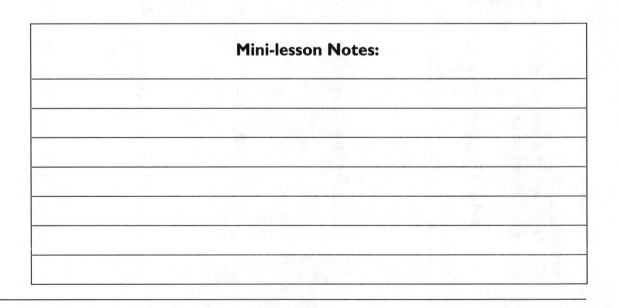

Mini-lesson Notes:

Literacy Center Connection:

Classroom Library: How to Use This Room!

Collect the student-made descriptions of the classroom. Have students add illustrations, or take photographs of the classroom and place the pictures on the appropriate pages. Add a table of contents and bind into a big book. Title the book *How to Use This Room!* and place a copy of the book in the classroom library.

Teaching Tip: At the Writing Center, students may create a *How to Use This Center* poster for each literacy center in the room. This will encourage student responsibility and ownership.

Lesson Variation and Notes:

- Place a different sticker on the back of each sentence strip. At each location in the classroom, place the corresponding sticker in an envelope for students to self-check. For example: Place a book sticker on the back of the question: *Where could I go to find Dr. Seuss books?* Then place a book sticker inside of the envelope at the Classroom Library to confirm the answer!

- Students can write the questions and have classmates identify the locations.

- Students can tackle *ALL* of the questions with a partner by completing the classroom scavenger hunt provided on page 100 or design their own scavenger hunt on page 101.

- When new students come to your classroom, have a "veteran" student take them on a tour of the classroom using these questions as a guide. Also, have them check out the class book titled, *How to Use This Room!*

How To Use This Room Scavenger Hunt

1. Where can I find books to read on my own?

2. Where can I find words to use in my writing?

3. Where can I find today's date?

4. Where can I find names of my friends?

5. Where can I find poems to read?

How To Use This Room
Scavenger Hunt

1. Where can I find _____ ?

2. Where can I find _____ ?

3. Where can I find _____ ?

4. Where can I find _____ ?

5. Where can I find _____ ?

Literacy Connection Planner
Using Features of Non-fiction Text to Find Information

Reading Strategy: Strategies for Finding Information

Materials: _____ Shared reading texts (use familiar Big Books with the features you will be highlighting in this lesson)
_____ Chart labeled *Features of Non-fiction*
_____ Markers
_____ Find the Feature recording sheet (page 105)

Mini-lesson:

Readers' Workshop Component: Shared Reading

1. Pre-select several familiar non-fiction titles. Think aloud about a feature of non-fiction: *When I want to find an answer to a question I have about spiders, I look at the Table of Contents of a book about spiders. The Table of Contents is found at the beginning of a book (show) and it tells me the page numbers I can turn to find information. In this book, the Table of Contents is found on page iii. Let's look closely to find out what we can learn from this book about spiders.*

2. Have students share what they learn from the table of contents. Record student responses on a chart labeled *Features of Non-fiction* (see chart, page 102).

3. Explain that the features of non-fiction are clues authors give us to help us locate information. Show a variety of non-fiction books with a Table of Contents and share how they can be used in different books.

4. Let students sort through a pile of non-fiction titles and find the books with a Table of Contents.

5. Revisit this lesson (and features of non-fiction chart) over time to introduce other features such as: index, glossary, bold typed words, captions, labels, charts and diagrams, etc.

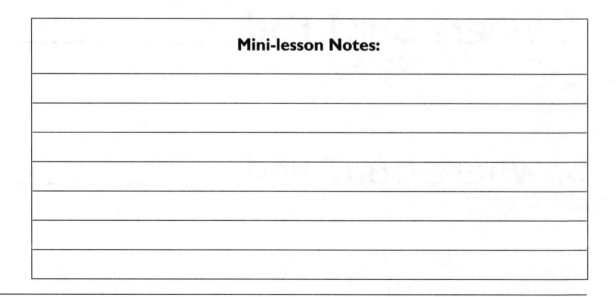

Mini-lesson Notes:

Literacy Center Connection:

Classroom Library: Find the Feature

Place several familiar non-fiction titles in the Classroom Library or Research Center. Place a chart titled "Find the Feature" in the center. Have students browse through books to find that feature and use the Find the Feature recording sheet on page 105 to list their discoveries.

Storage Tip: Laminate and Velcro the feature strips provided on page 104 to your chart. Use one strip at a time until students become more familiar with the features of non-fiction. Place the strips you are not using in a zipper storage bag and attach with a metal ring to the corner of your chart.

Lesson Variation and Notes:

- Store strips of highlighting tape on index cards at the center. Students can highlight the features of non-fiction as they find them.

- Adapt this idea for the Writing Center. Use your picture card file, post-its (for labeling) and Wikki Sticks (to connect labels to the picture) for students to create their own label diagrams

- Have students write their own captions to photographs in the picture file.

- When students are familiar with this concept, add more than one feature to your poster for students to find and record.

Features of Non-fiction chart Sample

Features of Non-fiction	How does it help me?
Table of Contents	Tells me what information is in the book and what page(s) I can turn to find it
Glossary	Tells me what specific words mean.
Bold Words	Tells me important vocabulary words and often has the definition following.
Labels	Shows me the names or parts of an object.
Charts/Diagrams	Helps me understand the topic and organize it in a different way.

Table of Contents

Glossary

Bold Words

Captions

Labels

Charts/Diagrams

Find the Feature

Name _____   Date _____

Feature	Title of Book(s)	Page #
Table of Contents		
Glossary		
Bold Words		
Captions		
Labels		
Index		
Charts/Diagrams		

Reading Connections

Strategies for Learning and Using Words - readers use their understanding of word identification and meaning during text interaction.

Page #	Mini-lesson Topic	Literacy Center Connection	Center Title
107	Activating prior knowledge to build vocabulary	Word Work	Lots of Lists
111	Using sound/symbol relationships to identify new words	Word Work	Stir the Stew
115	Building vocabulary through exploring words	Word Work	Vocabulary Calendar
120	Using new words in poems	Poetry	Poetry Notebooks

Literacy Connection Planner
Activating Prior Knowledge to Build Vocabulary

Reading Strategy: Strategies for Learning and Using Words

Materials: ____ Chart Paper
____ Markers
____ Shared reading text

Mini-lesson:

Readers' Workshop Component: Shared Reading

1. Share the title and author of the shared reading text with your students.

2. Ask students to share what they know about the topic. For example: If the book is about soccer ask, *What do you know about soccer?*

3. Generate and record student responses on chart paper. Make sure to record words as well as phrases. Help students make connections by pointing out how their responses are a result of what they already know.

4. Tell students to look for these words or phrases during the reading. When they locate a word or phrase stop briefly to acknowledge it.

5. After reading, discuss whether the author used the same words or phrases we listed. If not, did the author use different words (synonyms) that meant the same as our words? Did the author use different words and phrases than what we thought about?

6. If appropriate, add to the list.

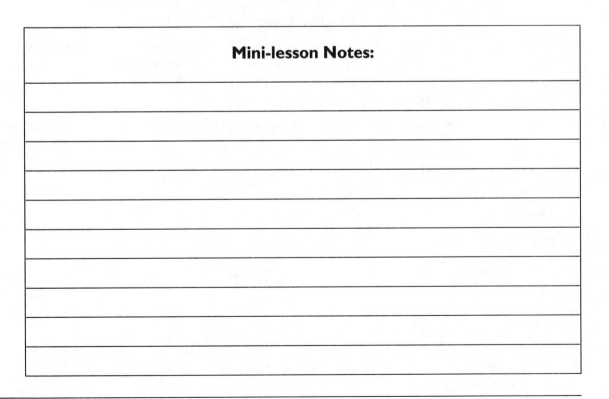

Mini-lesson Notes:

Literacy Center Connection:

Spelling/Word Work: Lots of Lists

On a wall in your spelling/word work center keep a poster labeled:

Lots of Lists
This week's topic:
_____

Change the topic weekly for students to generate their own lists of words or phrases related to the topic on adding machine tape. For younger students, put a picture next to the weekly topic for additional support. See page 109 for a list of possible topics.

Storage Tip: Use Velcro on the back of the topic strips for displaying on the poster. Have students store their lists in their writing folders to use for future writing topics.

Lesson Variations and Notes:

- Some children will need to create picture lists before they can start using words.

- Create a book titled *Our Class Book of Lists*. Label each page with a different topic and leave it in the center for your students to add to the lists. Some of the page labels could be: Pets, Favorite Names, Sports, Food, Rides at the Fair, Favorite Books, Names of Authors, etc.

- Listing is an important part of the writing process. As a follow-up mini-lesson, use a list generated by the students to make word cards. Sort and categorize the information into piles. Demonstrate how this can be used as a planner for writing.

- Have children take their personal lists and use them to categorize information when they visit this center. Later, they can choose one of their list sorts to expand into a writing piece.

55 List Topics

Beach Toys	Boy Names	Breakfast Food
Colors	Cold Things	Dr. Seuss Books
Family Members	Favorite Books	Farm Animals
Favorite Songs	Favorite Toys	Feelings
Foods I Love	Foods I Don't Like	Friends
Fruit	Furry Things	Games to Play
Girl Names	Green Things	Hard Things
Holiday Songs	Holiday Wish List	Hot Things
Ice Cream Flavors	In My House	Jobs
Musical Instruments	Ocean Animals	On the Ground
Places to Play	Places to Visit	Quiet Things
Rides at the Fair	Sand Toys	School Tools
Shapes	Smelly Things	Snack Food
Soft Things	Summer Things	Things in My Backpack
Things in the Sky	Things That Go	Tools
Vegetables	Ways We Move	Winter Things
Zoo Animals	_____	_____
_____	_____	_____

Lots of Lists Topic Cards

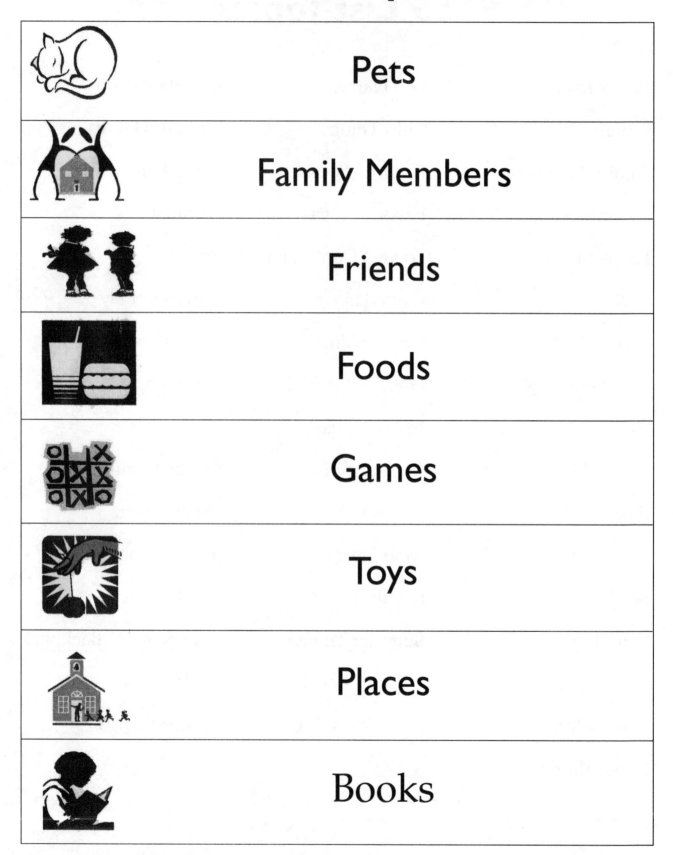

	Pets
	Family Members
	Friends
	Foods
	Games
	Toys
	Places
	Books

© 1999 Alonso & Nations *"Making Reading and Writing STICK"*

Literacy Connection Planner
Using Sound/Symbol Relationships to Identify New Words

Reading Strategy: Strategies for Learning and Using Words

Materials: ____ Shared reading text
____ Magnetic letters
____ Large bowl or soup pot
____ Soup ladle

Mini-lesson:

Readers' Workshop Component: Shared Reading

1. Choose one or two key words from your shared reading text.

2. Before showing students the book tell them you are going to turn the pages without reading while they look for tricky words. As they identify them, mark them with a sticky note or highlighting tape.

3. Read the text without stopping at the marked words.

4. Re-read the text. As you get to the tricky words stop to show them how to read all the way through the word. Stretch the sounds out with your mouth as you run your finger under each sound.

5. Choose one word to say as your students hold up fingers for sounds. Help them think out the word using what they know about letters.

6. Remind them there are many strategies for figuring out unknown words in text by thinking aloud: *I know there are lots of ways to figure out words that I don't know when I am reading. I sometimes look at the picture. Sometimes I skip it. Other times I get my mouth ready and it just pops out! When I use this strategy, I need to remember to let my eyes check and see that I am reading all the sounds in the word.*

7. Practice with some more words from the shared reading text.

Mini-lesson Notes:

Literacy Center Connection:

<u>Word Work: Stir the Stew</u>

Place magnetic letters in a bowl at your word work center. Pre-select the letters from words and word families you have studied. Provide a ladle to scoop out letters. Students can record the letters in their scoop. Challenge students to make words using only the letters they scoop out of the pot into a bowl. They can record their words on the reproducible bowl provided, or on adding machine tape.

Lesson Variation and Notes:

- Thanks to *Pat McCants, reading coach,* for this center idea. Pat has her young readers put on chef's hats and aprons as they participate in this center. Her kids have so much fun that she can't keep the "cooks out of the kitchen!"

- Keep lists of words posted in this center for students to use as a reference as they build words.

- Provide paper for students to record words they build and store in their writing folder. Use this as a record of student work in this center.

Possible Word-building Topics

Word families	Consonant clusters
Beginning sounds	Ending sounds
Digraphs	Plurals
Vowel sounds	Suffixes
Prefixes	Spelling words

Stir the Stew!

1. Stir the pot of letters.

2. Scoop some letters on your bowl.

3. Make as many words as you can from your letters.

4. Make a list of all the words you make.

Stir the Stew!

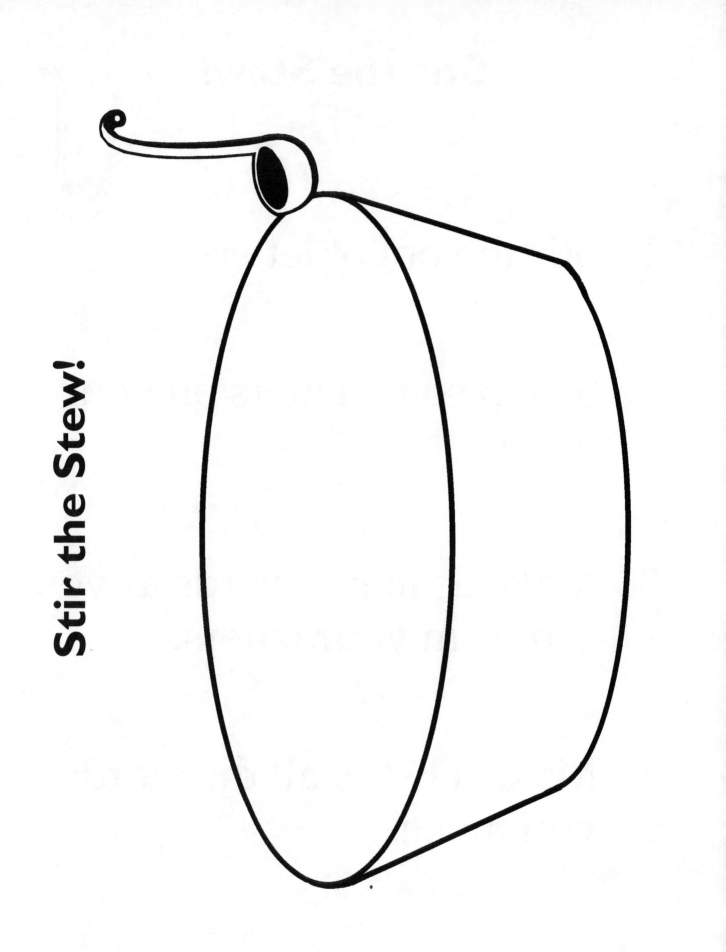

Literacy Connection Planner
Building Vocabulary Through Exploring Words

Reading Strategy: Strategies for Learning and Using Words

Materials: ____ Old calendars or computer-generated calendar (see page 119 to make your own)
   ____ Weekly calendar sheet (see page 118)
   ____ Paper
   ____ Pencils and markers

Mini-lesson:

Readers' Workshop Component: Shared Reading

1. Let your students brainstorm words that go with your current theme. For example, if you are talking about fall, the words might be autumn, red, yellow, orange, brown, leaves, cool, football, etc. Try to collect enough words to write one on each day of the calendar.

2. Say, *One of the ways we learn new words is to use them in many different ways. Today we are going to think of some ways we could play with these words by talking, writing, or reading them.*

3. Ask your students to brainstorm some things they might do with the words. For example: locate them in books, look them up in the dictionary, find another word that starts the same, alphabetize them, etc. After your students generate this list, model completing the activities by practicing some suggestions together.

4. Create a calendar of activities to work with your theme words in mini-lessons and at centers.

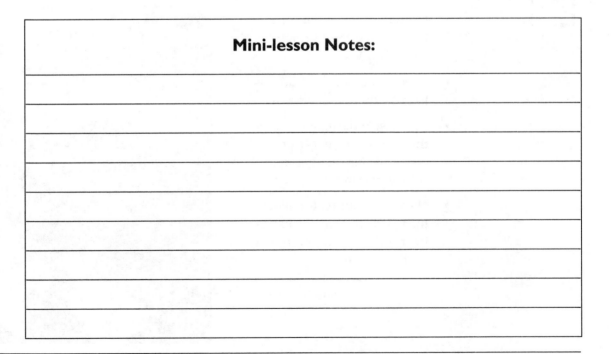

Mini-lesson Notes:

Literacy Center Connection:

Word Work: Vocabulary Calendar

Place a monthly calendar in your word work center. Label each day with a word that you will be discussing during the month. Display a weekly activity calendar next to the monthly calendar. Label each day with a word that matches your theme or topic of study for the month.

Also display a weekly calendar with activities to use the words. See sample Vocabulary Calendar with activity cards on page 117.   Here is a list of possibilities:

- Read all the *Monday* words to a friend

- Read and write all the words that start with ____.

- Put all the words in week *one* in ABC order.

- Look up *four* interesting words in the dictionary.

- Write all the words that have *two syllables*.

- Write *three* words in a sentence.

- Find *two* words in a book.

- Write all the words that have long ___ sound.

- Read all the *nouns* to a friend.

- Find some words that have the letters in *your name*.

- Write the words that are on *even* days.

- Read the words that can describe something.

Lesson Variations and Notes:

- Display the calendar on a tri-fold board with rings. See example.

- Keep a notepad for students to carry out the day's task.

- Purchase old calendars after the first of the year from discount stores or garage sales to use in this center.

- Have your students collect the words they might use in their writing and put in their writing folder.

Sample Vocabulary Calendar
with Activity Cards

May						
Sun	**Mon**	**Tue**	**Wed**	**Thu**	**Fri**	**Sat**
1 ocean	2 whale	3 pod	4 spout	5 krill	6 mammal	7 water
8 fish	9 dolphin	10 swim	11 crab	12 octopus	13 blue	14 green
15 reef	16 coral	17 shell	18 shore	19 wave	20 sand	21 tide
22 salty	23 manatee	24 stingray	25 starfish	26 sail	27 fin	28 lobster
29 urchin	30 oyster	31 swim				

Week of: May 1-7		**Week of May 8-14**	
Monday:	Read all the Monday words to a friend.	Monday:	Write all the words with more than one part.
Tuesday:	Write all the words with a short vowel.	Tuesday:	Read week one and two to a friend.
Wednesday:	Put week one's words in ABC order.	Wednesday:	Write all the words with a long vowel sound.
Thursday:	Choose 8 words to sort. Ask a friend to guess your sort.	Thursday:	Choose 3 words to write in sentences.
Friday:	Read all the words with one part to a friend.	Friday:	Read all the Friday words to a friend.

Week of:				
Monday	Tuesday	Wednesday	Thursday	Friday

Week of:				
Monday	Tuesday	Wednesday	Thursday	Friday

Month: _____

Sun	Mon	Tue	Wed	Thu	Fri	Sat

Literacy Connection Planner
Using New Words in Poems

 Reading Strategy: Strategies for Learning and Using Words

Materials: ____ Chart poems from shared reading
____ 3" x 5" Sticky Notes
____ Spiral notebook (one per child)
____ Tape
____ Markers, crayons, pencils

Mini-lesson:

Readers' Workshop Component: Shared Reading

1. Pre-select several familiar poems you have written up on large charts or overhead transparencies. Cover words on the charts that can be changed with sticky notes. (Hint: the rhyming words in a poem are easy to change and often can change the meaning of the poem entirely.)

2. Have your students brainstorm lists of words that could fit on each sticky note.

3. As a class select one sticky note to replace each covered word. Read the poem together. Talk about the new meaning.

4. Remind your students that poems are meant to be read aloud and enjoyed over and over again. Tell them they will each begin keeping a poetry notebook of familiar poems they learn in class. This notebook sometimes will be used to help make new poems for the class to read.

I like spiders!	I like whales!
Black spiders, brown spiders	Orca whales, Blue whales
Spin a web that's round spiders.	Even make the news whales.
Big spiders, scary spiders,	Big whales, jumping whales,
Small gray and hairy spiders	Water-splashing humpback whales
Old spiders, striped spiders	Beluga whales, large whales
No matter where they hide spiders,	Even as big as a barge whales,
I like spiders!	I like whales!

Mini-lesson Notes:

Literacy Center Connection:

Poetry: Poetry Notebooks

After your students learn a poem well, copy it onto small sheets of paper and place in the Poetry Center. Students should practice reading the poem to a friend. When they know it, they can tape the poem into a spiral-bound poetry notebook and illustrate it. Encourage older students to number their pages and record their poems in a table of contents (see page 123). Students continue to add to these notebooks throughout the year. At the end of the year, your students will have a very special anthology of poems to remember this grade.

Lesson Variations and Notes:

- Use tape to attach poems in the notebooks. Glue is sometimes messy and pages get stuck together.

- Send the poetry notebook home once a quarter for students to read to their family. Parents can write a special note in the notebook about the poems. (See note on page 122)

- Young children can start by making a poetry notebook of nursery rhymes and simple poems.

- Encourage students to put poems they find during independent reading in their poetry notebooks.

- Students can refer to their notebooks during Writer's Workshop when they look for examples of author's craft.

- Keep your own poetry notebook as a reference.

Dear Parent,

Today your child is bringing home his/her poetry notebook. Each week we learn many new poems in class. These are often posted in our room, and the children practice reading them on their own during our literacy center time. This helps young readers build fluency in reading.

After your child has learned a poem well enough, it will be put into the poetry notebook for him/her to illustrate and read to a friend.

On the last Friday of each month your child will bring the notebook home to share with you. Please listen to him/her read the new poems. Then take a minute to write a note about what you heard. You can share what you liked about the poems or the reading your child did. The poetry notebook should be returned on Monday so he/she can start working in it again.

As always, thank you for your support as we help your child become a lifelong reader!

Sincerely,

My Poetry Notebook Table of Contents

Page #	Poem Title	Author

Writing Connections

Strategies for Building Fluency and Independence - writers self-select topics and write for a variety of purposes.

Page #	Mini-lesson Topic	Literacy Center Connection	Center Title
126	Writing for an audience	Writing Center	Writing Ideas Poster
128	Setting the mood for writing	Listening Center	Music, My Pencil, and Me
130	Writing with a purpose in mind	Writing Center	Pen Pals
132	Recording words from reading to use later in writing	Writing Center	Personal Word Walls

Literacy Connection Planner
Writing for an Audience

Writing Strategy: Strategies for Building Fluency and Independence

Materials: ____   Chart poem *Writing Ideas* on page 127
                 ____   Pointers
                 ____   Samples of different types of writing

Mini-lesson:

Readers'/Writers' Workshop Component: Shared Reading

1. Think aloud: *Today I am going to read you a new poem about writing. This poem helps me remember about all the different types of writing I can do. It is titled Writing Ideas.*

2. Read the poem aloud.

3. Ask students to identify the different types of writing in the poem. *How many can we find in our classroom?* Help students identify different types of writing already in the classroom. Let them know you are going to post the poem near the writing center to help them remember the different types of writing they might try.

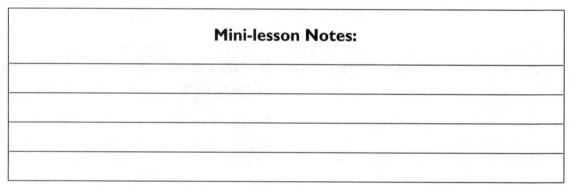

Mini-lesson Notes:

Literacy Center Connection:

Writing Center: Writing Ideas Poster

Post the poem near your writing center to help students when they need a writing idea. If possible, place student writing of each type near the poem. Rotate these samples occasionally to help keep students ideas fresh.

Lesson Variations and Notes:

- Students can add their own ideas or verses to the Writing Ideas Poem.

- Students can create their own small book of the Writing Ideas Poem to keep in their writing folder or to take home.

- Students can use the poem as a check list of ideas to try. As they try each type of writing they can put a check mark over it.

Writing Ideas

Write a letter.

Write a song.

Make a list—

short or long.

Write a riddle,

or a book.

All you need to do is look
All around you, my oh my…
There are hundreds of
writing ideas to try!

Susan Nations

Literacy Connection Planner
Setting the Mood for Writing

Writing Strategy: Strategies for Building Fluency and Independence

Materials:
_____ CDs or tapes of relaxing music
_____ CD or cassette player
_____ Paper and pencils
_____ Timer (optional)

Mini-lesson:

Writer's Workshop Component: Independent Writing

1. Explain to your students that when writers write they often work many days or months to finish a book or piece of writing. It is important that they get all their ideas out on paper and then go back and decide what to keep and what not to keep. They often have a specific place they write or music they listen to while writing.

2. Say, *Today we are going to practice writing while we listen to music. This may help some of you who say you don't know what to write. You might find the music helps you put words on your paper as you relax and think.*

3. Encourage your students to find a comfortable space to write. They may want to lay on the floor with a clipboard or pillow.

4. Make sure everyone has an idea of what to write about before you put on the music. Play the music for three to five minutes while the students write.

5. Discuss how it felt to write with the music. Was it hard? Easy? Did the music make a difference? If so, what?

6. Allow your students to work on this piece of writing for several days in the same way.

7. During the longer portion of Writer's Workshop, conference with your students individually or in small groups about their writing.

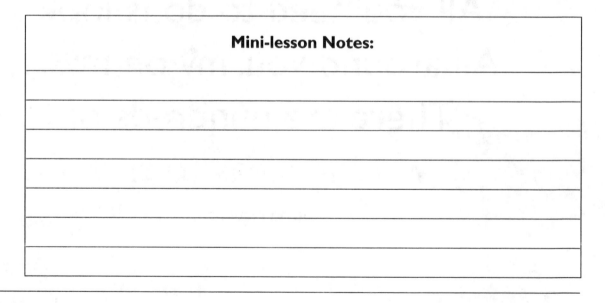

Mini-lesson Notes:

Literacy Center Connection:

Listening Center: Music, My Pencil and Me

Provide several CDs or cassettes with relaxing instrumental music in your listening center. Students will need paper and pencil along with their writing notebooks to complete this center. Invite students to select music to listen to while writing. For added creative stimulation, put a plant, pillows and a lamp in this center. Have students share the writing they produce during whole group sharing time or display it on a bulletin board titled, "Music, My Pencil, and Me."

Lesson Variations and Notes:

- Classical music will help students use their creativity in writing.

- Ask your music teacher to help with musical selections.

- Many stores stock nature CDs with soothing music and nature sounds.

- Encourage students to revisit previous writing for possible revision when they are in this center.

- You may want to purchase inexpensive personal tape players for students to use at their seats while writing.

Literacy Connection Planner
Writing with a Purpose in Mind

Writing Strategy: Building Fluency and Independence

Materials:
____ Index cards or postcards
____ Markers
____ Stickers (to be used as "stamps")
____ Poster board or chart paper

Mini-lesson:

Writers' Workshop Component: Modeled Writing

1. Revisit a familiar story about writing letters. (Examples – *Letters from Felix, The Jolly Postman*)

2. Share postcards or letters you have received from friends or family and discuss the similarities (date, greeting, body, closing)

3. Discuss how postcards can be used to send messages to friends in order to communicate. Display an enlarged example of a "postcard."

4. Share how the front side of a postcard usually displays a picture and the back of the postcard has space for writing.

5. Using your enlarged copy, think aloud as you model write: *Today I have chosen to write a postcard to my best friend Michelle. I will write "Dear Michelle" for the greeting. I want to tell her about our field trip to the zoo.* (begin writing as you talk aloud) *"Yesterday, I went to the zoo with my friends. We saw a monkey, an elephant and many kinds of birds. Other animals were taking their naps. Have you ever been to the zoo?" Notice how I ended my postcard with a question. I did this so Michelle will want to write back with an answer. Now I will write a closing, "Your Friend, Mellissa."*

6. Give students their own copy of a postcard to write a note to a friend. Conference with individuals or small groups as they write.

7. Encourage students to end their postcard with a question for their friend to answer.

8. Model how to stamp and address a postcard on the next day.

Mini-lesson Notes:

Literacy Center Connection:

<u>Writing Center: Pen Pals</u>

Place materials at the Writing Center that encourage letter or postcard writing. Stock the center with envelopes, post cards, index cards, stickers, mailboxes, pens, markers, etc. Place examples of letters and postcards in the center for students to use as a reference.

From Mellissa:

At Temple Terrace Elementary, my first grade class paired with Mike Meiczinger's second grade. We helped students form pen pal partners. Our classes would send post cards to each other once a week. Mike contacted our local post office for curriculum ideas and center materials for our Writing Center. The students were motivated to respond to their pen pals as they learned the history of our mail delivery system.

Lesson Variation and Notes:

- Contact your local post office for launching a Post Office Center in your classroom.

- Create individual mailboxes from shoeboxes, cereal boxes, cardboard dividers, etc.

- Visit your local discount store and purchase your own mailbox.

- Place your teacher mailbox in the center for students to write to you.

- Display related literature titles about pen pals and letter writing in the center.

Literacy Connection Planner
Recording Words from Reading to Use Later in Writing

Writing Strategy: Building Fluency and Independence

Materials: ____ Familiar read aloud, Big Book or poem
____ Highlighting tape
____ Personal Word Wall (enlarged version or transparency copy)
____ Markers

Mini-lesson:

Writers' Workshop Component: Shared Writing

1. Revisit a familiar read aloud, Big Book or poem.

2. Think aloud, *Sometimes I need to borrow words other authors have used in my writing. It helps if I have a place to write these words down so I can use them later in my own writing.*

3. Display an enlarged version (or transparency) of the Personal Word Wall example.

4. Have students help you locate words you may want to use in your writing at a later time. Use highlighting tape to find the words, then model how to record them on the Personal Word Wall.

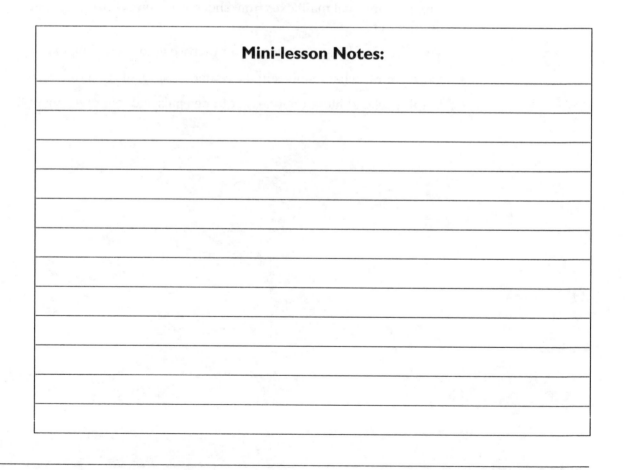

Mini-lesson Notes:

Literacy Center Connection:

Writing Center: Personal Word Wall

Make a tri-fold from two file folders. Staple each sheet of the Personal Word Wall to each side of the tri-fold. Make a Personal Word Wall for each student. At the center, have students record words from text that they have read. During writing time, encourage students to use the Personal Word Wall as a resource for spelling and word choice.

Lesson Variation and Notes:

- Words captured on the Personal Word Wall may be individualized for each student.

- Encourage students to record words not found on the class word wall.

- Words may include: high frequency words, hard-to-spell words, interesting words or phrases, etc.

- Copy the attached Word Wall sheets on pages 134, 135, and 136 or design you own.

Aa

_____

_____

_____

_____

_____

_____

_____

_____

_____

Bb

_____

_____

_____

_____

_____

_____

_____

_____

_____

Cc

_____

_____

_____

_____

_____

_____

_____

_____

_____

Dd

_____

_____

_____

_____

_____

_____

_____

_____

_____

Ee

_____

_____

_____

_____

_____

_____

_____

_____

_____

Ff

_____

_____

_____

_____

_____

_____

_____

_____

_____

Gg

_____

_____

_____

_____

_____

_____

_____

_____

_____

Hh

_____

_____

_____

_____

_____

_____

_____

_____

_____

Ii

_____

_____

_____

_____

_____

_____

_____

_____

_____

Jj

_____

_____

_____

_____

_____

_____

_____

_____

_____

Kk	Ll	Mm	Nn	Oo

Pp	Qq	Rr	Ss	Tt

Uu	Vv	Ww	Xx	Yy
_____	_____	_____	_____	_____
_____	_____	_____	_____	_____
_____	_____	_____	_____	_____
_____	_____	_____	_____	_____
_____	_____	_____	_____	_____
_____	_____	_____	_____	_____
_____	_____	_____	_____	_____
_____	_____	_____	_____	_____

Zz				
_____	_____	_____	_____	_____
_____	_____	_____	_____	_____
_____	_____	_____	_____	_____
_____	_____	_____	_____	_____
_____	_____	_____	_____	_____
_____	_____	_____	_____	_____
_____	_____	_____	_____	_____

Writing Connections

Strategies for Communicating a Message - writers construct text for a variety of purposes.

Page #	Mini-lesson Topic	Literacy Center Connection	Center Title
138	Identifying an audience and purpose for writing	Writing Center	Student Message Book
142	Writing good beginnings and endings	Listening	Listen for the Lead
146	Writing to inform	Writing	Extra! Extra!
150	Using complete sentences in writing	Research Center	Help Wanted—Job Applications

Literacy Connection Planner
Identifying an Audience and Purpose for Writing

Writing Strategy: Strategies for Communicating a Message

Materials: ____ Chart paper or overhead projector
____ Markers
____ Individual student message books

Mini-lesson:

Writers' Workshop Component: Modeled Writing

1. Create a large student message book using chart paper or overhead transparencies.

2. Arrange students so they can see your writing model.

3. Begin with a think aloud such as: *Before I write, I think about who will be reading my writing. Will it be my teacher? My Mom? My friend? Today I have decided I am going to write a message to my friend, Jordan. Before I do that, I need to think about what I want to say to him. I want to tell him about my pet dog, Corky. I am going to do this by writing him a letter in his student message book. I need to find his student message book in the box in our writing center. When I open the book, I need to turn to the first blank page. I will begin writing at the top of the page. I need to begin my letter to Jordan with the words, "Dear Jordan,"*

Model writing a letter on the chart paper or overhead projector so students can observe the process. Draw attention to specific word choice such as "Dear Jordan,", "Your Friend", etc. to demonstrate your awareness of the audience (your friend) and purpose for your writing.

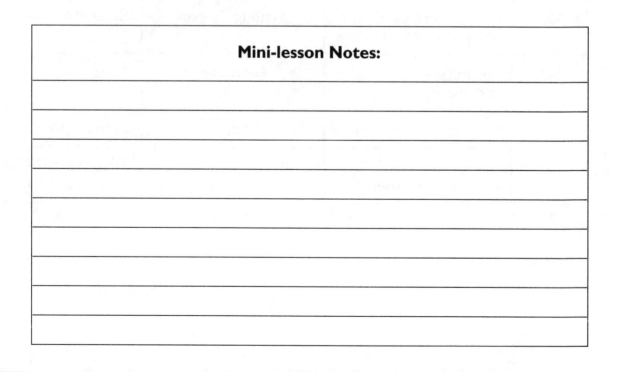

Mini-lesson Notes:

Literacy Center Connection:

<u>Writing Center: Student Message Books</u>

Make a message book for each student in your classroom. This can be done with a piece of construction paper and newsprint stapled into a booklet or a folder with blank pages in the middle. Label the books _____'s *Message Book* or use the covers provided on page 140. For added interest, have students decorate their own front covers. After conducting the mini-lesson, place the message books in your writing center. Students can write messages to each other when they are in the writing center.

<u>Storage Tip</u>: Store the message books in a file box or shoe box in alphabetical order.

Lesson Variations and Notes:

- Set up writing buddies for the student message books to ensure that all students will receive messages in their books.

- Use a three-ring binder to be a class message book. Fill the notebook with tabbed dividers labeled with your students' names. When one student wants to write a message, she can turn to that person's section and write in the next available space. Occasionally take individual student pages out of the binder and staple them together to send home.

- Introduce the concept of letter writing using literature such as *Letters From Felix* by Langen and Droop or *The Jolly Postman* by Janet and Alan Ahlberg.

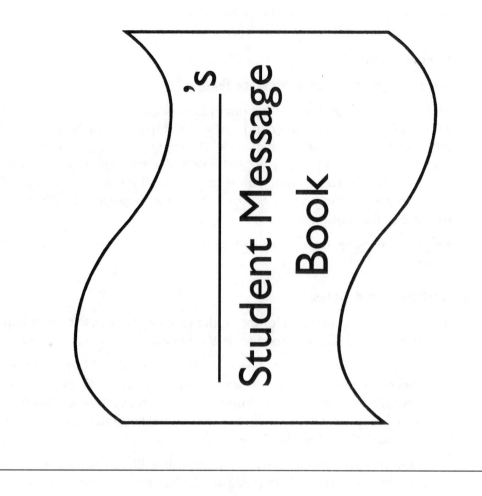

_____'s

Student Message
Book

_____'s

Student Message
Book

When you write a message, don't forget:

Dear (<u>Your friend's name</u>),

    The body of your message should be what you want to say.

    At the end, write a closing like this:

Your Friend,
(<u>Your Name</u>)

Literacy Connection Planner
Writing Good Beginnings and Endings

Writing Strategy: Strategies for Communicating a Message

Materials: ____ Books and articles with good beginnings and endings
____ Examples of writing without a good beginning or ending

Mini-lesson:

Writing Workshop Component: Modeled and Independent Writing

1. Say, *Listen while I read some beginnings and endings to you from some books and articles in our classroom library.*

2. Share several with your students and ask them to identify those that are most appealing. Discuss why. *Is it the descriptive language? Alliteration? Strong verbs? Rhythm? Rhyme?*

3. Share some that are not as strong and discuss the difference.

4. Model revising a weak lead or ending with a prior piece of writing of your own. Talk to students about how you choose words that you think will appeal to your reader in your writing. Share with your students why you selected this lead or ending as your model.

5. Invite students to take out a piece of writing from their writer's notebook to try writing a strong beginning or ending.

6. Assist students in this process with one minute mini-conferences as they work.

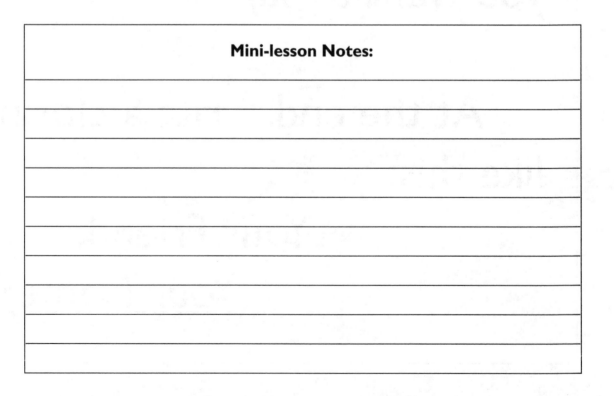

Mini-lesson Notes:

Literacy Center Connection:

<u>Listening: Listen to the Lead/Ear for Endings</u>

Pre-record several leads and endings for students to listen to in your listening center. When possible, provide a copy of the book or articles you use for student reference. Encourage students to bring a piece of their own writing with them to the center to consider revision possibilties. Don't forget to use some of your own student writing as samples. Keep these tapes available for students to use throughout the year.

Lesson Variation and Notes:

- As students locate good beginnings/endings during their reading, encourage them to practice their fluency and record it for other students to use in this center.

- With young children begin with the lead as your focus. After they get plenty of practice noticing and using leads in their writing, make endings the focus in this center.

- Have students occasionally add a lead or ending to a bulletin board, Writer's Craft Log, or poster for community use.

> **From Mellissa:** I kept a bulletin board labeled *Leading the Way to Better Writing* for my first grade students to record good leads. As they located good leads in text, they would write them on construction paper books cut out of my school's die cut machine. We would display them for student reference during writing workshop.

Listen to the Leads

1. Choose a cassette tape.

2. Find the books or articles in the basket that you will hear on the tape.

3. Listen to the leads.

4. Write any that sound good to you.

5. Try one in your own writing.

6. Share your work with a friend.

An Ear for Endings

1. Choose a cassette tape.

2. Find the books or articles in the basket that you will hear on the tape.

3. Listen to the endings.

4. Write any that sound good to you.

5. Try one in your own writing.

6. Share your work with a friend.

Literacy Connection Planner
Writing to Inform

Writing Strategy: Communicating a message

Materials: _____ Recent copies of your morning message (about 10 days)
_____ Overhead transparency of page 148

Mini-lesson: Writing to share with others

Writer's Workshop Component: Shared Writing

1. Collect at least two weeks' worth of morning messages before beginning this lesson.

2. Discuss what kinds of information gets written in the morning message (birthdays, news from the classroom, what we will be learning, activities we will be doing, etc.)

3. Re-read several of your morning messages to locate the above information in your messages. Ask, *What might other people learn about our classroom if they read our messages?*

4. Think aloud: *Our morning message reminds me of reading the newspaper. Sometimes it tells me about things that have already happened in class. Other times I learn about what is going to happen. We also find interesting information about our classmates in our morning message.*

5. *We want our parents and other people to know about our classroom. How could we use our morning messages to make a classroom newsletter?* Have the students give you suggestions.

6. Use the template on page 148 to make an overhead transparency to continue with a shared writing of your current classroom news.

7. After you complete it, put it in a sheet protector and let your students read it during center time at your overhead.

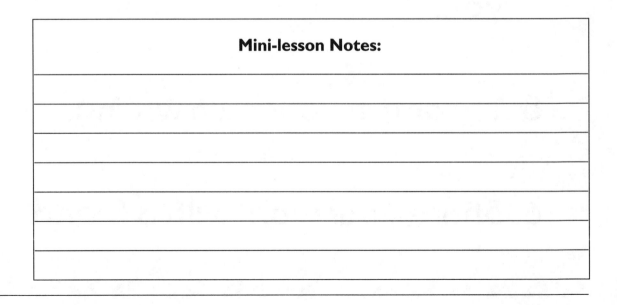

Mini-lesson Notes:

Literacy Center Connection:

Writing Center: Extra! Extra!

Have your students create a classroom newsletter using your morning messages. You can assign specific children to be the authors of designated sections of the newsletter. After they have written their section, it should be turned in to you for final editing. Consider asking a parent volunteer to type it up on the template. Distribute to your parents and other school personnel regularly. Bind all the classroom newsletters into a notebook for students to read all about it!

Note: You may want to make a center that is separate from your writing center called *The News Desk*. This would be the place where your classroom newspaper is written. Only the news crew on assignment can use it.

Lesson Variations and Notes:

- Keep a suggestion box in your classroom for students to submit things they would like to see in the classroom newsletter.

- If your school doesn't announce morning messages, conduct a shared writing lesson with your class using the template for noteworthy events. Gradually add to it until you have enough news to send it home.

- Rotate your writers in the same way you rotate other classroom jobs. You could even create an assignment chart for your young reporters. (See page 149)

_____' Class News

This Week At School		What We're Learning (Themes and Things)
	Celebrations	

New and Noteworthy	Reading —
	Writing —
	Math —

This Week's Reporters:

This Week at School:

_____

Celebrations:

_____

What We're Learning:

_____

New and Noteworthy:

_____

Reading:

_____

Writing:

_____

Math:

_____

Literacy Connection Planner
Using Complete Sentences in Writing

Writing Strategy: Communicating a Message

Materials: ____ Writing samples
____ Overhead transparency or enlarged chart of page 152
____ Markers
____ Small copies of job applications for students (see pages 153 and 154)

Mini-lesson:

Writers' Workshop Component: Modeled Writing

1. Read some writing with incomplete sentences. Ask students *what is wrong with what I read?* Help children discover that it doesn't make sense.

2. Talk about how the reader wants to hear the whole sentence so it makes sense.

3. Say, *when you write it is important that you write in whole sentences. If you only put part of the words in a sentence, you will leave your reader guessing what you are trying to say.*

4. *Today we are going to practice writing in whole sentences. I would like to talk to you about a special type of writing we are going to start called a job application. Let's think together about all the jobs we have here in our classroom.* Record students responses on chart paper.

5. Display a large copy of a job application and model filling it out using complete sentences to answer each question.

6. Explain to students that each week they will have the opportunity to apply for a classroom job. Remind them that their application must have complete sentences in it.

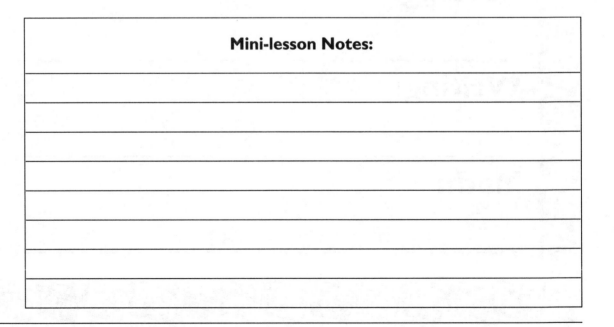

Mini-lesson Notes:

Literacy Center Connection:

Research Center: Help Wanted - Job Applications

Make a small book of each job in your classroom. Keep blank job applications in an envelope at the center. Children may apply for one job each week. They must explain why they want the job and how they plan to do it. Younger children may start out by drawing a picture and labeling it with the job title on it.

Lesson Variations and Notes:

- Teacher *Linda Long* uses weekly job applications with her first grade students. Her students learn quickly to write legibly and to highlight their strengths when they apply for jobs.

- Photograph a student doing each of the assigned jobs in your classroom. Label these photos with the job title and place in the center for students to use as reference.

- If weekly applications are too much for you and your students, consider having one week a month where students apply. During the other weeks, rotate student names as usual.

Help Wanted

⇨ Choose a job card.

⇨ Read about the job and decide why you want it.

⇨ Fill out the application for the job.

⇨ Use your best handwriting!

Line Leader

- Walks quietly in line
- Helps lead the class when walking around the school
- Sets an example for others in line

Door Holder

- Holds the door when the class is entering and exiting
- Shuts off the lights when all classmates are out of the room
- Makes sure the door is closed quietly behind the last person

Materials Manager

- Helps pass out materials to be used in class
- Makes sure materials are being used properly
- Puts materials away neatly when the class is done using them

Caboose

- Walks at the end of the line when the class is moving around the school
- Makes sure all classmates are in the line
- Helps the door holder if necessary
- Walks quietly in line

Light Monitor

- Turns lights off when class is leaving the room
- Makes sure lights are on when the class returns
- Checks bathroom lights before leaving for the day

Messenger

- Delivers messages to and from the office if necessary
- Walks in the hallways
- Helps teacher give messages to other classmates or classrooms

Calendar Helper

- Helps with calendar time each morning
- Makes sure date is written on the board
- Checks date stamps in centers for correct date

Lunch Money and Attendance

- Collects lunch money to be put in the envelope
- Helps teacher know who is absent
- Delivers lunch money and attendance to office

Name: _____ Date _____

What classroom job would you like to do _____

_____

Why?

_____

_____

Name: _____ Date _____

What classroom job would you like to do _____

_____

Why?

_____

_____

Name: _____ Date _____

What classroom job would you like to do _____

_____

Why?

_____

_____

Name: _____ Date _____

What classroom job would you like to do _____

_____

Why?

_____

_____

Writing Connections

Strategies for Using Information - writers communicate their discoveries for a variety of purposes and audiences.

Page #	Mini-lesson Topic	Literacy Center Connection	Center Title
158	Identify a purpose for writing	Research	Food For Thought
160	Gathering and recording information	Research	Student Surveys
166	Using questions to gather information	Research	Phone a Friend
170	Using details in writing	Writing Center	Focus Frames

Literacy Connection Planner
Identify a Purpose for Writing

Writing Strategy: Strategies for Using Information

Materials: _____ Food boxes and labels
_____ Chart paper and markers

Mini-lesson:

Writers' Workshop Component: Shared Writing

1. Collect enough identical food boxes for groups of four to share.

2. Begin by noticing attributes of the text and layout of information on the food box. For example: *I notice that this food box has a lot of writing on it. The name of the food is in very large and colorful letters. I notice there is a picture of what is inside the box. I think this is to make me want to buy it. When I look at the words I see that it describes ways to use this product. I can even find places where the writers want me to see the reasons I should buy it.*

3. Have the groups look at their boxes to locate the same types of information. After each group has come up with a few ideas have them share with the rest of the class.

4. Record the words, phrases or specific details that make the buyer want to purchase this food. Display this chart in the Research Center.

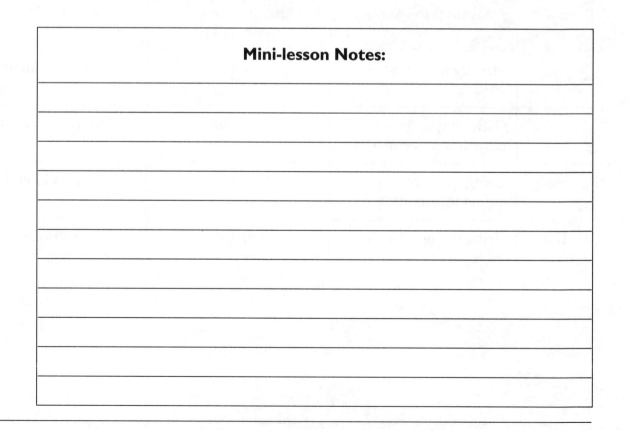

Mini-lesson Notes:

Literacy Center Connection:

Research Center: Food For Thought

Place a variety of food boxes and labels in the Research Center. Students choose one to read about. They need to look at all the information that is located on the box or label. Students make a list of words, phrases, or details to add to the chart.

Storage Tip: Flatten the food boxes by cutting off the top and bottom. Store them in a gallon-size resealable bag.

Lesson Variation and Notes:

- Food boxes provide a rich supply of research and problem-solving possibilities. Locate numeric information and create math word problems for your students to solve.

- After a mini-lesson on using charts, graphs or tables ask students to locate some on the food boxes. Let them work with a partner to read and interpret the information.

- Younger students can use the food boxes to locate colors, shapes, words, letters, etc.

- Follow the same procedure as identified in Attraction Action on page 87 and create question cards to be posted in this center.

- Have students sort and classify a variety of food boxes. There are many possibilities for sorting: healthy/non-healthy, food groups, refrigerated/non-refrigerated, etc. Let students come up with their own sort and explain their rationale.

- Locate recipes on food boxes for students to use applied reading and following directions skills. They can read the recipe and record in a learning log how they would make it.

- To regenerate this center and keep it fresh have students bring in food boxes throughout the year to complete the above activities.

> From Susan: My first-grade students enjoyed making books out of food boxes. They collected cereal boxes and used the binding machine to make them into a book. This provided a source of environmental print for those students who were emergent readers.

Literacy Connection Planner
Gathering and Recording Information

Writing Strategy: Strategies for Using Information

Materials: ____ Survey questions printed on sentence strips
____ Clipboards
____ Paper and pencil
____ Highlighters

Mini-lesson:

Writer's Workshop Component: Shared Writing

1. Ask your students, *Which do you like better, hot dogs or hamburgers?* Let them show you by a raise of hands.

2. Informally tally up the votes and make a statement, such as *In our class, more girls like hot dogs and more boys like hamburgers.*

3. Say, *When I find out information about our class, it is called a survey. I am finding out what you think about something. Then I can make an observation about the information I have, like when I said, 'More girls like hot dogs and more boys like hamburgers.' This is a way of reporting information.*

4. *If I want to write what I learned in my survey, I could have you sign your names under the column that shows which you like better.* Write down how many of your students like hot dogs and how many like hamburgers.

5. *Then I could use this information to write what I learned at the bottom. What could we say about our survey?*

6. Have students help you come up with one or two sentences about the survey. They can help you write the words they know. Students can also share the pen with you. They come up write a letter they know in the word and you add any missing letters with another pen.

7. Re-read your message and connect back to the original survey.

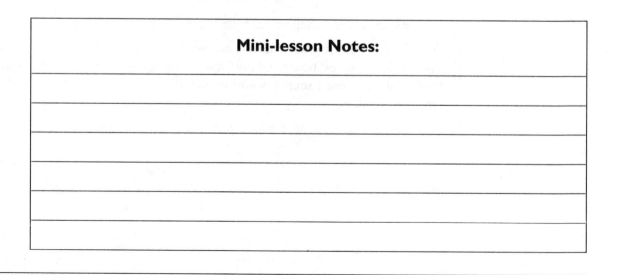

Mini-lesson Notes:

Literacy Center Connection:

Research Center: Student Surveys

Make a survey poster. On one side divide it in half for two-answer surveys and on the other side divide it into four. Post a daily or weekly survey question for your students to record. Teach your students to respond to the survey in the column that best fits their answers. Young children can write their name on a sticky note and put it under their survey answer. When the survey is complete, let students in the research center use their clipboards and interpret the survey data. Use the list of survey topics on page 162 to help you.

Lesson Variations and Notes:

- Keep a box in your research center for students to submit survey suggestions they would like to use in class.

- Use student interpretations of the survey for assessment purposes.

- Have students use the sentence stems from the Reader's Response Chart on page 86 to discuss the survey results.

- Use catalogs, newspaper advertisements, and old worksheets as picture sources for your survey topics.

Student Surveys

Two-Column Surveys (Yes or No)

- Do you like apples? Yes, No
- Have you been in an airplane? Yes, No
- Do you have a pet?
- Do you like _____?
- Have you seen _____?
- Have you read _____?
- Do you have a bicycle? Yes, No
- Which is your favorite book? (Choose two recent read alouds)
- Did you like the end of the book?

Do you eat spinach?	
Yes	No
Bob	Scott
Patti	Linda
Kevin	

Which toy do you like best?			
Yo-yo	Ball	Puzzle	Game
Margi	Brenda	Juan	Callie
Jon	Don	Linda	
	Amy		
	Errol		

Three or Four Column Surveys

- How do you get to school? Car, Bus, Walk, Ride
- How many people in your family? Two, Three, Four, Five+
- What color are your eyes? Blue, Brown, Black, Green
- Which is your favorite apple color? Red, Green, Yellow
- Which animal do you like best?
- Which is your favorite food (drink, dessert, etc.)?
- Who is your favorite character?
- Which picture is your favorite? (Post four pictures on your survey board)

Surveyor: _____ **Question:** _____

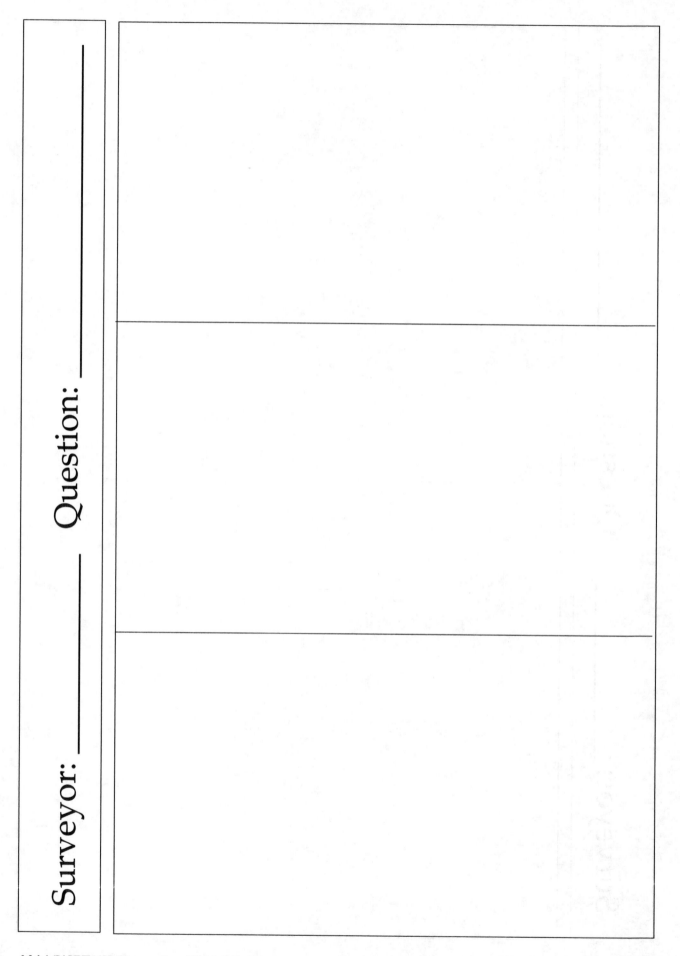

Question: _____

Surveyor: _____

Surveyor: _____

Question: _____

Literacy Connection Planner
Using Questions to Gather Information

Writing Strategy: Strategies for Using Information

Materials: ____ Chart paper and markers
____ Interview questions
____ Clipboards
____ Play phones
____ Notepads or paper for the interview

Mini-lesson:

Writing Workshop Component: Shared Writing

1. Good writers ask questions to find out information as they write. Ask your students to help you think of questions to ask if you want to write about a person you know. Record their responses on chart paper.

2. Try using the questions to find out about someone at school. If possible try to use another familiar adult in your school to model this with you.

3. After the interview, ask the students if there are any other questions they want to add. If so, record them on the chart and ask the person being interviewed.

4. Talk about how you can now use the information to write about this person. Write a paragraph or two with your students to model the process.

Note: This lesson may take several days to complete.

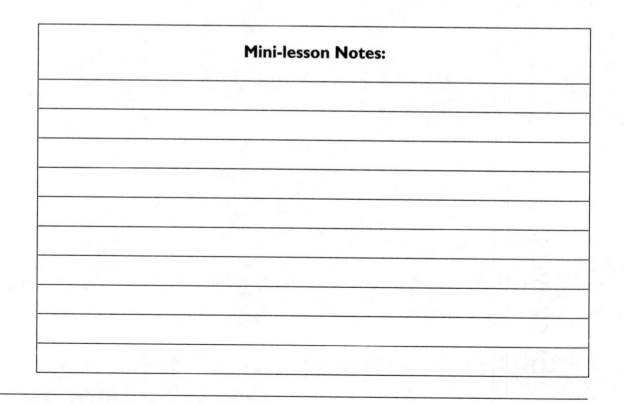

Mini-lesson Notes:

Literacy Center Connection:

<u>Research: Phone a Friend</u>

Place the interview question chart along with two play phones in your research center. Students can use this chart as they phone their friend and interview them.

For a fun project with your students create a *Phone a Friend* big book. Pair your students and ask them to interview each other. The interviewer should write a paragraph using the information learned without using the name. Bind these descriptions in a class big book. On each page attach a library pocket or flap with the name of the interviewed student underneath. Your class will love reading the descriptions and seeing if they can guess who each page is about.

Lesson Variations and Notes:

- Occasionally change the questions students ask. This helps build community in the classroom as you learn about each other.

- Provide clipboards and pencils for note-taking during the interview.

- Your students can create autobiographical paragraphs by answering the questions individually. Compare the content with the paragraph the interviewer writes and discuss what makes them different.

- Send your students out into the building to interview school personnel. Bind this into a book called *People in My School.* Share this book with new students enrolled in your class during the year.

Phone a Friend

I talked to: _____

I learned: _____

_____

_____

_____

Phone a Friend

I talked to: _____

I learned: _____

_____

_____

_____

Sample Phone a Friend Questions

- What is your name?
- Where were you born?
- Do you have a pet? Tell me about it.
- Where is your favorite place to visit?
- What is your favorite food?
- When is your birthday?
- What is your favorite sport?
- Who is your favorite author?
- What is the best book you ever read?
- What do you like to do for fun?
- How long have you been in our school?
- What do you like best about our school?
- What is your favorite holiday?
- What are your family's special celebrations?
- What is your favorite song?

Literacy Connection Planner
Using Details in Writing

Writing Strategy: Strategies for Using Information

Materials: ____ Frames of various sizes (see pages 172-173)
____ Overhead trasparencies of frames in at least two sizes
____ Overhead transparency of picture or large picture from a magazine or poster

Mini-lesson:

Writer's Workshop Component: Shared Writing

1. Hold up a picture all of your students can see. Ask them to think about what they notice in the picture. After giving them a moment to think, let them share with a partner what they notice.

2. Overlay a large Focus Frame on the picture and ask, *Now what do you notice? Is there anything different this time?* Discuss with a partner

3. Use the smaller focus frame to zero in on a detailed section of the picture. Help your students notice the details in the frame now. They should describe it to their partner.

4. We can notice details in many places. Give each pair of students a frame and let them find an object or picture in the classroom to describe either verbally or in writing.

5. Let students share what they noticed in their frame. Say: *When writers write, they look for small details to make their readers more able to see what is happening in the writing. Let's look for some ways writers give us good strong details in the books we read.* Let students notice or discuss details they remember from reading workshop titles.

6. It is fun to take these frames along with clipboards and writing paper outside to practice describing details found in the school yard.

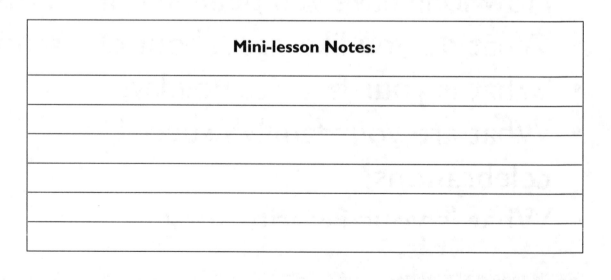

Mini-lesson Notes:

Literacy Center Connection:

<u>Writing Center: Focus Frames</u>

Place a box of laminated focus frames in a variety of sizes in your writing center. Students can use these during writer's workshop or literacy centers to notice details to use in their writing. For an extra challenge, have students write their details on an index card. Other students can read the cards and see if they can guess the picture and identify the part where the writer was trying to focus in his writing.

<u>Storage Tip:</u> Consider hole-punching several sizes of focus frames and attaching them to a book ring. Students can pick up a ring and take several frames with them to use during writing practice.

Lesson Variations and Notes:

- Collect a set of focus-frame writing for assessment. Students should be very clear about what they notice in the pictures. Young children should be able to get one or two strong details in their writing.

- Use wordless picture books and have students attend to details using the focus frame. These books can be placed in the focus-frame box for use during writing center.

- Collect pictures from *National Geographic, Ranger Rick, Zoobooks*, etc. for students to use in this center.

- Have older children pair up with a picture. Make sure the pictures you choose show action. Let student A look at the picture while the student B cannot see it. Student B should ask questions about the picture while student A gives details about the picture. Student B should try to guess what is happening in the picture.

Focus Frames

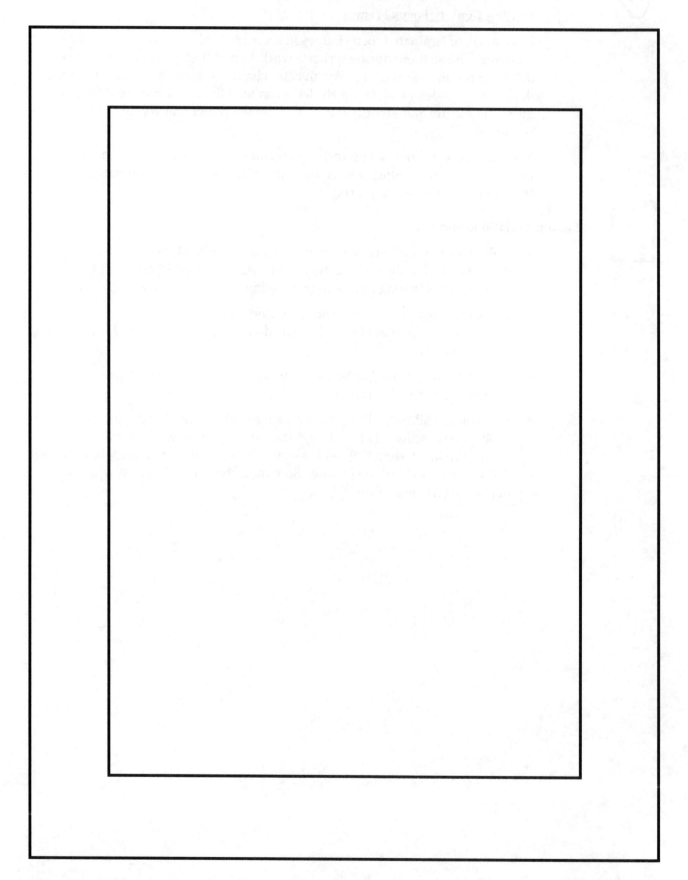

Focus Frames

Writing Connections

Strategies for Word Choice - writers use their understanding of words and their meaning to make effective word choices.

Page #	Mini-lesson Topic	Literacy Center Connection	Center Title
176	Noticing author's use of craft in text	Classroom Library	Writers' Craft Catchers
178	Engaging the reader using descriptive details	Writing Center	Write the Room
180	Identifying unknown words by word patterns	Research	What's My Sort?
183	Finding and using names of people in writing	Word Work	Make My name

Literacy Connection Planner
Noticing Author's Use of Craft in Text

Writing Strategy: Strategies for Word Choice

Materials: _____ Familiar read-aloud books from the classroom library in a variety of genre

Mini-lesson:

Writers' Workshop Component: Shared Writing

1. Begin by thinking aloud about a specific type of author's craft, such as:

   When I read a book, I notice that the author uses tricks to keep me interested. We have talked about some of these tricks such as: similes, metaphors, talking to the reader, etc. Today we are going to look at the hooks that an author uses to get the reader into the book or article.

2. Give each student a book or article from your classroom library.

3. Ask them to look at the opening line or two of the book or article. Talk about what words the author chose and why.

4. Record student's findings on a class chart labeled *Writer's Craft: Great Hooks*

5. After students have added to the list as a group, invite them to add to the list as they discover good hooks during their independent reading.

6. You may repeat this same mini-lesson each time you want to focus on a new aspect of author's craft.

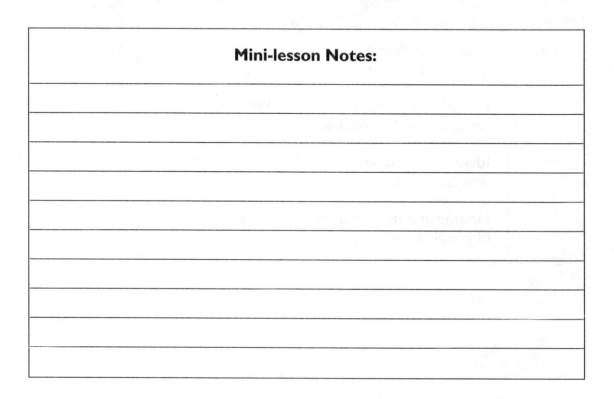

Mini-lesson Notes:

Literacy Center Connection:

Classroom Library: Writer's Craft Catchers

Create a small book labeled *Writer's Craft: We've Noticed*... and place it in your classroom library. Encourage students to use it to add their discoveries of the author's craft they find during their reading time. From time to time, make this book a part of your writer's workshop as you look at writing craft. Add new pages to the center book as you locate more examples of authors' craft during writer's workshop. Remind students that when they are looking for a good idea, it is ok to imitate the pros. This book can become a reference for students to use as they work on their own writing.

Lesson Variations and Notes:

- Younger children may not be able to notice and record the craft that authors use on their own. You can continue to use this mini-lesson to visit other examples of strong writing during your read aloud time. As you model and notice new components of strong writing, create and label new charts for students to use as a reference.

- With young writers you might change the name of your log to Writer's Patterns We've Noticed. Help them notice different patterns authors use such as: ABC, rhyme, rhythm, numerical, circle, etc. Record titles together during read aloud and shared reading.

- Students could keep a Writer's Craft page in their writing folders. When they notice beautiful language, good leads, strong verbs etc. they can record it in their own folders for use during independent writing.

- Older students enjoy highlighting specific word choice in newspaper or magazine articles for strong verbs, color words, precise nouns, etc.

- For more information on target skills and strong writing see Marcia S. Freeman's books: *Building a Writing Community* or *Teaching the Youngest Writers* and Ralph Fletcher's *Craft Lessons*.

Literacy Connection Planner
Engaging the Reader Using Descriptive Details

Writing Strategy: Strategies for Word Choice

Materials: ____ Clipboards
____ Highlighters
____ Papers
____ Poems and charts posted around the room

Mini-lesson:

Writers' Workshop Component: Modeled Writing

1. Show students the clipboards with highlighter attached.

2. Say to the students:

   Good writers are always noticing the words and phrases around them. When they read something they like, they will often write it down. I am going to look around our room for words and phrases that I like. When I find one, I am going to write it down. Maybe someday I will use it in my writing.

3. Model the process of finding words and phrases that you like posted on your classroom or in books you have read. Talk about how these phrases engage you as a reader.

4. Record the phrases on your paper as you talk about how you may go back and use this information someday.

5. Use the highlighter to mark important words or phrases that you like. Explain to students that highlighting helps you see the important words quickly.

Mini-lesson Notes:

Literacy Center Connection:

Writing Center: Write the Room

Provide plenty of clipboards and paper in your writing center. Explain to students that it is there for them to write the room. They can find words and phrases they like and record them. Remind them to put completed papers in their writing folders so they can revisit them during writers' workshop.

Lesson Variations and Notes:

- Store clipboards in a box clearly labeled *clipboards*. Attach highlighters with a string.

- Occasionally use the Write the Room for students to find words and phrases with specific elements. For example, they may write strong verbs they find, words with the same spelling pattern, parts of speech or other types of writers craft.

- Post a sign that shows what the focus is for write the room each week.

Possible Write the Room Topics

Words that start with _____.

Words that end with _____.

Color or number words

Comparisons

Strong Verbs

Good descriptions

Words or phrases I like

Beautiful language

Good hooks/endings

Questions

Names

Literacy Connection Planner
Identifying Unknown Words by Word Patterns

Writing Strategy: Strategies for Word Choice

Materials: ____ Word cards from a familiar read aloud/shared reading
____ Sorting tray (plastic relish trays with dividers work well)
____ Other items to sort
____ What's My Sort? Worksheet

Mini-lesson:

Writers' Workshop Component: Word Work

1. *Think about words that you have tried to write but didn't know how to spell. What did you do? Did any of you ask a friend or teacher? Did anyone go to the dictionary? One thing I do when I don't know how to spell a word is think about how it might look. In my mind I think about other words I know that sound the same or almost the same. For example, if I want to spell the word train, I think about the words I know that sound like train like rain and plain. Then I try it out on a piece of paper to see if it looks right.*

2. Show your students how to try spelling a word in three different ways and pick one. For train you might write *trane, tran,* and *train.* Then help them to see how you think about what might be the right spelling.

3. Your choice may not be right, but this is a good way to try and spell. Most of the time you will be able to figure it out, or at least get close enough until you can check it somewhere else.

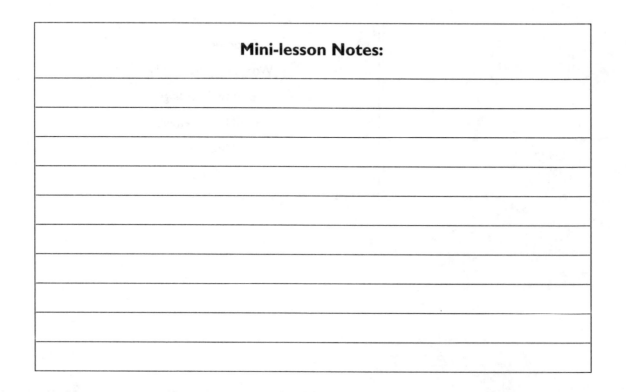

Mini-lesson Notes:

Literacy Center Connection:

Research: What's My Sort?

Explain to your students that this center is in the research center because it focuses on noticing similarities and differences in words or things. Remind students of the mini-lesson where you thought about words that were alike to help you spell in your writing. Place several word cards in your research center. These words can come from your big books, guided reading books, word wall, spelling lists, etc. Provide a divided paper or plastic serving tray for students to sort the word. They need to find a friend and have them guess how the words were sorted. Occasionally replace the words with other small objects to be sorted.

Lesson Variations and Notes:

- Coordinate your sort with letter study. For example, when you are studying "M words" consider sorting colored macaroni.

- Novelty catalogs often sell items in bulk that are excellent for sorting.

- Ask parents to help you collect items to sort.

Some Sorting Ideas

Alphabet cereal
Beads
Buttons
Coins (real or plastic)
Crayons (peel and use the broken ones)
Coupons
Flower pictures (use the seed catalog)
Food boxes and labels
Grocery coupons, gift wrap
Insects (plastic)
Jingle bells
Keys
Matchbox cars
Marker caps (save the ones from dried up markers)
Nuts and bolts
Pasta in a variety of shapes
Quilt squares (make out of paper)
Rocks
Seeds
Sea shells
Small Toys
Words
Yarn in various lengths and colors
Zippers (from your local sewing center)

Things I notice about

_____ 's sort:

_____

_____

_____

_____

_____

_____

Things I notice about

_____ 's sort:

_____

_____

_____

_____

_____

_____

Things I notice about

_____ 's sort:

_____

_____

_____

_____

_____

_____

Things I notice about

_____ 's sort:

_____

_____

_____

_____

_____

_____

Literacy Connection Planner
Finding and Using Names of People in Writing

Writing Strategy: Strategies for Word Choice

Materials: _____ Chart paper
_____ Index cards with students names
_____ Magnetic letters
_____ Aluminum cookie pan

Mini-lesson:

Writer's Workshop Component: Independent Writing

1. Talk to your students about how writing changes as you get older. Explain that when you are young, you are still learning words to use in your writing. Say, *Today I am going to show you how my writing has changed since I was your age.*

2. Begin by scribbling on the board and saying, *When I was little, my writing looked like this: _____. It looked that way because I didn't know how to spell or make letters.*

3. Continue with: *When I grew older, I learned how to spell my name like this: Susan. Then when I wanted to write, I could put all of the letters from my name in my writing.*

4. *When I grew a little older, I learned to spell my friend Michelle's name. I wrote a lot about my friend Michelle and I playing in our neighborhood.*

5. Ask students to locate places in the room where they might find the names of other classmates. Explain that they will write about a friend during writing time.

6. Give each child a sticky note and a pencil. Let them find their friend's name in the room and copy it onto the note to be used during writing workshop. They should store these sticky notes in their writing notebook for future reference.

Mini-lesson Notes:

Literacy Center Connection:

Word Work: Make My Name

Make a small dictionary of names of all the students in your class. If possible, use their pictures to support your young readers. Bind them with a key ring or comb binding. Store these in your Word Work center. Students can choose any medium to recreate other students' names. They might use Play Dough, Wikki Sticks, pipe cleaners, markers, or letter tiles.

Lesson Variations and Notes:

- Have students record three names on a sticky note they might use in their writing. These should be kept in their writing notebook.

- Use the Recording Sheet on page 186 to have all students sign. Copy these for each student to keep in the writing notebook.

- After students have used the dictionary in the Word Work center, move it to the Writing Center to encourage letter writing.

- Create other word dictionaries for your centers using old worksheets, stickers, and pictures.

- Make a book of characters' names from shared reading and read aloud texts.

25 Things to Do with Kids' Names

Sort them
by letter
by syllable
by length
Rainbow-write them
Remake them with new medium (pipe cleaner, marker, etc.)
Scramble them and play Guess Who?
Put them in ABC order
Write a letter to someone
Stamp them out
Make new words out of them
Make an autograph book
Look for them in books
Compare two or more: what's the same? different?
Make an address book
Go on a name hunt in the classroom and tally them
Find them in books and magazines
Make a wall of fame for kids to post their names when
they know how to write it
Match them
Choose a pictograph for it
Make a flip book out of it
Cut them out of magazines
Match them with pictures of people
Play Name Concentration
Write a sentence
Try all this with last names

My friends at school. . .

_____   _____

_____   _____

_____   _____

_____   _____

_____   _____

_____   _____

_____   _____

_____   _____

_____   _____

_____   _____

_____   _____

_____   _____

Appendix

Standards for the English Language Arts

by the International Reading Association and the National Council of Teachers of English

Copyright 1996 by the International Reading Association and the National Council of Teachers of English. Reprinted with Permission.

The vision guiding these standards is that all students must have the opportunities and resources to develop the language skills they need to pursue life's goals and to participate fully as informed, productive members of society. These standards assume that literacy growth begins before children enter school as they experience and experiment with literacy activities—reading and writing, and associating spoken words with their graphic representations. Recognizing this fact, these standards encourage the development of curriculum and instruction that make productive use of the emerging literacy abilities that children bring to school. Furthermore, the standards provide ample room for the innovation and creativity essential to teaching and learning. They are not prescriptions for particular curriculum or instruction.

Although we present these standards as a list, we want to emphasize that they are not distinct and separable; they are, in fact, interrelated and should be considered as a whole.

1. Students read a wide range of print and nonprint texts to build an understanding of texts, of themselves, and of the cultures of the United States and the world; to acquire new information; to respond to the needs and demands of society and the workplace; and for personal fulfillment. Among these texts are fiction and non-fiction, classic and contemporary works.

2. Students read a wide range of literature from many periods in many genres to build an understanding of the many dimensions (e.g., philosophical, ethical, aesthetic) of human experience.

3. Students apply a wide range of strategies to comprehend, interpret, evaluate, and appreciate texts. They draw on their prior experience, their interactions with other readers and writers, their knowledge of word meaning and of other texts, their word identification strategies, and their understanding of textual features (e.g., sound-letter correspondence, sentence structure, context, graphics).

4. Students adjust their use of spoken, written, and visual language (e.g., conventions, style, vocabulary) to communicate effectively with a variety of audiences and for different purposes.

5. Students employ a wide range of strategies as they write and use different writing process elements appropriately to communicate with different audiences for a variety of purposes.

6. Students apply knowledge of language structure, language conventions (e.g., spelling and punctuation), media techniques, figurative language, and genre to create, critique, and discuss print and nonprint texts.

7. Students conduct research on issues and interests by generating ideas and questions, and by posing problems. They gather, evaluate, and synthesize data from a variety of sources (e.g., print and nonprint texts, artifacts, people) to communicate their discoveries in ways that suit their purpose and audience.

8. Students use a variety of technological and information resources (e.g., libraries, databases, computer networks, video) to gather and synthesize information and to create and communicate knowledge.

9. Students develop and understanding of and respect for diversity in language use, patterns, and dialects across cultures, ethnic groups, geographic regions, and social roles.

10. Students whose first language is not English make use of their first language to develop competency in the English language arts and to develop understanding of content across the curriculum.

11. Students participate as knowledgeable, reflective, creative, and critical members of a variety of literacy communities.

12. Students use spoken, written, and visual language to accomplish their own purposes (e.g., for learning, enjoyment, persuasion, and the exchange of information).

Glossary of Terms

Authentic Response – Responding to text in meaningful and purposeful ways selected by the reader.

Conferencing – Spending time with students helping them talk, question and think their way through reading and writing experiences. Can be done one on one or in a small group with similar need.

Content Area Materials – Text that is specific to non-fiction genre such as math, science and social studies.

Expectations – Reading and writing behaviors students should be able to demonstrate.

Genre – Literature classifications such as poetry, fiction, non-fiction, biography, etc.

Literacy Block – time allocated daily for reading and writing instruction, guided and independent practice. Should be consistent each day.

Mini-lesson – Brief teacher-directed demonstrations focused on student need.

Open-ended – Responses or activities that allow for creativity, varied level of need, and individuality.

Skills – Pieces of information the learner can apply during strategy use.

Standards – Guidelines established to measure a student's understanding of a subject area and provide a framework for instruction at each grade level.

Strategies – Processes the learner knows how and when to access during reading and writing; meaningful application of skills.

Self-monitor – The ability for a student to manage reading and writing tasks successfully and to be aware when the literacy process breaks down.

Writer's Craft – Writing techniques authors use to engage a reader.

Literacy Connection Planner

 Reading Strategy:

Materials:

Mini-lesson:

    Readers' Workshop Component:

Literacy Center Connection:

 Lesson Variations and Notes:

Literacy Connection Planner

 Writing Strategy:

 Materials:

 Mini-lesson:

Writers' Workshop Component:

Literacy Center Connection:

Lesson Variations and Notes:

Research

Literature Response

Writing

Poetry

Reading

Word Work

Read the Room

Listening

Poetry Center

Writing

Literature
Response

Research

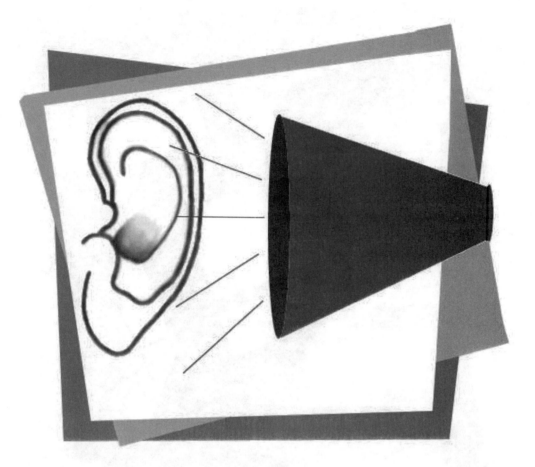

Listening
Center

Read the Room

Word Work

Reading Corner

Literature Response Matrix Explanations

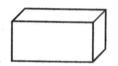 Retelling Box – Students fill a box or bag with props or drawings that will help retell the story to the class or group.

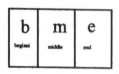 BME Sheet – Students paste a b, m, and e on the page and illustrate or write the beginning, middle and end of the story.

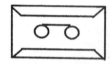 Tell a Tape – Students may use the tape recorder to read their favorite part of the book.

 Create a Cover – Students create a new cover for the book and include information and details.

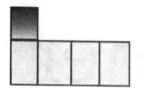 Four Flap Book – Students make a four-flap book to record events from a story or information from a book they read.

 Buddy Reading – Students pair up to read all or a portion of their book.

Write a Letter – Students can write a letter to a character in their book. They can also write a letter to a friend telling them about the book.

Write Questions – Students record questions as they read. Keep a list of question stems available to help them.

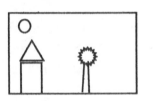

Sketch a Scene – Students sketch their favorite scene from the book. They can share it during book talks or display it in the room.

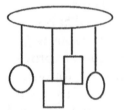

Make a Mobile – Students can use scraps to make a mobile of events, characters, or story elements from the book.

Find Fun Facts – Students use nonficiton text to locate facts about a topic.

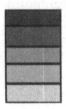

Step Book – Students use this book to record events, vocabulary, steps in a process, or other information about the book.

One Final Note from Mellissa and Susan

We first met in 1995 during a twelve-week professional development seminar on early literacy. Each week we wrestled both individually and in small groups with how children acquire reading and writing skills. Later that year, we were asked by our district to attend an intensive two-week summer course on early literacy. It was there that we became response journal partners and discovered how much there was to learn and how much fun it is to process with a fellow educator!

Each afternoon the instructional part of the course stopped for professional reading time. We were to record in a notebook our learning and response to our independent reading. When we came back together we had to share our responses with our partner. Thus began the written and verbal dialogue which would propel our growth as educators and friends.

During those early exchanges we realized that we wanted so much more for our classrooms, our students, and our professional selves. Our response log continued long after the two weeks was over. We corresponded through the school mail (this was

prior to email!) as we devoured professional title after professional title. This is something we continue to this day via email and phone calls.

It is that journey we began so many years ago that brings us here today. This book allows us to share what worked in our classrooms with you. Most of what is in these pages are activities and lessons we discovered as we made our quest to provide quality early literacy experiences for our students. It continues for each of us as we share our learning in staff development and training of elementary educators around our districts and the country.

We believe that professional growth is a process that does not end. There is so much new learning out there regarding teaching and learning almost daily! *Primary Literacy Centers* is a book that records our learning about giving young children meaningful learning experiences in the language arts classroom. We realize, however, that this is but a step on our journey as we continue to learn and grow. We hope this book will be an important part of your journey as you seek to meet the needs of the students you teach.

Professional References and Resources

Bodrova, Elena, and Deborah J. Leong. 1996. *Tools of the Mind: The Vygotskyian Approach to Early Childhood Education.* Englewood Cliffs, NJ: Prentice-Hall.

Calkins, Lucy, Kate Montgomery, and Donna Santman, with Beverly Falk. 1998. *A Teacher's Guide To Standardized Reading Tests: Knowledge Is Power.* Portsmouth, NH: Heinemann.

Cambourne, Brian. 1988. *The Whole Story:Natural Learning and the Acquisition of Literacy In The Classroom.* New York: Ashton Scholastic.

Cooper, J.D. 2000. *Literacy: Helping Children Construct Meaning* 4th ed. Boston, MA: Houghton Mifflin.

Clay, Marie. 1993. *An Observation Survey of Early Literacy Achievement.* Portsmouth, NH: Heinemann.

Fisher, Bobbi. 1998. *Joyful Learning in Kindergarten.* Rev. ed. Portsmouth, NH: Heinemann.

_____. 1995. *Thinking and Learning Together: Curriculum and Community in a Primary Classroom.* Portsmouth, NH: Heinemann.

Fleming, M. 1998. *Poem of the Week.* New York: Scholastic Professional Books.

Fletcher, R. 1998. *Craft Lessons: Teaching Writing K-8.* York, ME. Stenhouse.

Fountas, Irene C., and Gay Su Pinnell. 1996. *Guided Reading: Good First Teaching for All Children.* Portsmouth, NH: Heinemann.

Freeman, Marcia S. 1995, 1998. *Building a Writing Community: A Practical Guide.* Gainesville, FL: Maupin House.

_____. 1998. *Teaching the Youngest Writers: A Practical Guide.* Gainesville, FL: Maupin House.

Gentry, J. Richard. 2000. *The Literacy Map.* Greenvale, NY: Mondo Publishing.

Goldish, M. 1994. *Animal Poems From A to Z.* New York: Scholastic Professional Books.

Healy, J. 1990. *Endangered Minds: Why Children Don't Think and What We Can Do About It.* New York: Simon & Schuster.

Holdaway, Don. 1979. *The Foundations of Literacy.* Sydney: Ashton Scholastic, distributed by Heinemann, Portsmouth, NH.

Instructor Books. 1983. *Poetry Place Anthology.* New York: Scholastic.

Keene, Ellin L. & Susan Zimmerman. 1997. *Mosaic of Thought: Teaching Comprehension in a Reader's Workshop.* Portsmouth, NH: Heinemann.

McCarrier, A., Gay Su Pinnell, and I. Fountas. 2000. *Interactive Writing: How Language & Literacy Come Together, K-2.* Portsmouth, NH: Heinemann.

Mooney, M.1990. *Reading to, with, and by Children.* Katonah, NY. Richard C. Owen.

Moore, H. 1997. *A Poem a Day.* New York: Scholastic Professional Books.

Parkes, B. 1999. Talk Given at Florida Reading Association Conference. Orlando, FL.

_____. 2000. *Read It Again! Revisiting Shared Reading.* York, ME. Stenhouse.

Routman, Regie. 2000. *Conversations, Strategies for Teaching, Learning and Evaluating.* Portsmouth, NH: Heinemann.

_____. 1994. *Invitations: Changing as Teachers and Learners K-12.* Portsmouth, NH: Heinemann.

Wong, Harry & Rosemary Tipi Wong. 1988. *How to Be an Effective Teacher: The First Days of School.* Mountain View, CA: Harry K. Wong Publications.

Children's Literature

Raschka, C. 1994. *Yo! Yes!* New York: Orchard.

Fletcher, R. 1997. *Twilight Comes Twice.* New York: Clarion.

Cannon, J. 1993. *Stellaluna.* San Diego: Harcourt Brace.

Rylant, C. 1985b. *The Relatives Came.* New York: Scholastic.

Langen, A. and C. Droop. 1994. *Letters From Felix.* New York: Abbeville Publishing.

Ahlberg, J and A. Ahlberg. 1986. *The Jolly Postman.* Boston: Little Brown.

Brown, Margaret Wise. 1977. *The Important Book.* New York: Harper Collins.

Stewart, Sarah. 1997. *The Gardener.* New York: Farrar, Straus, Giroux.

Watts, Jeri Hanel & Felicia Marshall. 1997. *Keepers.* New York: Lee & Low Books.

Newbridge Educational Publishing. 2000. *Thinking Like a Scientist Series.* Delran, NJ.

A Quick-Reference Guide to Finding Specific Center Activities in *Primary Literacy Centers*

Index

Elementary, My Dear!

Jane Bell Kiester
Caught'ya! for Grades 1-3

Enhance early success in language arts for all students. Teaches basic, grade-appropriate skills in context. A story each for grades 1, 2, and 3, plus an extra chapter filled with writing ideas to help students achieve success on standardized tests. All classroom-proven. **$19.95**

$24.95 - with computer disk of the first-grade story formatted in Word, one sentence to a page for individual student journals. Specify MAC or PC when ordering.

Literature Models to Teach Expository Writing

Susan McElveen and Connie Dierking
For K-5 teachers

Model and demonstrate target-skill concepts central to expository writing with quality children's literature. Teach description, explaining how and why, leads and endings, cause and effect, comparing and contrasting, and fact and opinion. Three levels of lessons—kindergarten, primary, and intermediate—allow you to customize lessons to the competency levels of your students. Includes step-by-step directions, charts, and a recommended list of other literature that illustrates the expository target skills. Helps you integrate writing throughout your curriculum. By the authors o*f Teaching Writing Skills with Children's Literature.* **$23.95**

Snipper Critters
Easy Art Activities to Stimulate Language Across the Curriculum

Mary Doerfler Dall
For K-3 teachers

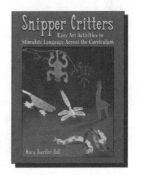

Unusual animal patterns from A to Z combine with activities to use the animals in social studies, science, math, and writing. Includes a bibliography of picture books, with natural history of each animal, plus ways to group the animals to teach across the curriculum. **$17.95**

1-800-524-0634 • www.maupinhouse.com